PRIZEWINNING LITERATURE

UK literary award winners

PRIZEWINNING LITERATURE

UK literary award winners

Anne Strachan

THE LIBRARY ASSOCIATION
LONDON

© Anne E. Strachan 1989

Published by
Library Association Publishing Ltd
7 Ridgmount Street
London WC1E 7AE

All rights reserved. No part of this publication may be photocopied, recorded or otherwise reproduced, stored in a retrieval system or transmitted in any form or by any electronic or mechanical means without the prior permission of the copyright owner and publisher.

First published 1989

British Library Cataloguing-in-Publication Data

Strachan, Anne E.
 Prizewinning literature: UK literary award winners.
 1. English literature. Prizewinning books
 I. Title II. Library Association
 820.9

ISBN 0-85365-558-8

Typeset in 9/10pt Univers by Library Association Publishing Limited
Printed and made in Great Britain by Bookcraft Ltd, Midsomer Norton, Avon.

For my mother, who started this particular ball rolling, and to Sue and all the others who assiduously read their way through many of the books in these lists raising money for Oxfam as they did so.

Contents

Preface	ix
Introduction to the guide	xi
Index to the prizes	xii
List of prizes	1
New prizes	231
Author index	232
Subject index	262
Bibliography	266
Useful addresses	267

Preface

In 1964 Tom Maschler, addressing a meeting of the Society of Young Publishers on the subject of literary prizes, said 'most of us have heard of these prizes, but I doubt if many of us, publishers, critics or public know who the previous award winners have been'.[1] By the late 1980s, though the winning titles and authors of the larger prizes are given much publicity in the media, there was still no full retrospective list to enable the adult general reader to capitalize on this upsurge of interest in good literature. This guide has been produced to fill that gap.

Not all the books listed here will be judged by everyone worthy of an award, but for each title not enjoyed there will be many others which will make the search worthwhile. This book can supplement the other important means of widening one's reading and finding personal favourites from the use of serendipity in the library or bookshop to finding interesting-looking titles under hotel beds or buying the only book from a station stall that will squeeze into the last of one's luggage space.

---

[1] *Bookseller* 7 November 1964, 1966–70.

Introduction to the Guide

This guide is intended to be as up-to-date as possible at the time of publication. The entries have been compiled from information sent by the administrators of the awards and prizes and I apologize in advance for any inaccuracies and would be grateful if these could be brought to my attention.

It was not the intention to list every literary award. The rationale behind the guide is as follows:

1   It is intended for the adult general reader: hence awards for children's literature and those for works which require a specialist subject knowledge have been excluded.

2   Only current awards are listed.

3   Awards based in the United Kingdom only have been included though the winning authors may be citizens of other countries.

4   The winning titles must be relatively easy to obtain hence awards for unpublished manuscripts have been excluded unless publication in book form is guaranteed by the award.

Details of those awards which fall outside the scope of this guide can be found in the books listed in the bibliography at the end.

Entries are listed in chronological order and as most of the awards are for books published in the previous calendar year the date given is the date when the award was presented rather than the year in which it was published.

The entries give the original edition (usually hardback) unless there is a subsequent edition in print. Paperback (pbk) and large print editions (large print ed.) are given if they are in print. Editions in print at the time of publication of the present volume are marked with an asterisk *. ISBNs or BNB numbers are given when these can be traced but for works earlier than 1950 only the publisher and the date of publication are given.

In May 1990, the 01– London telephone code will change to 081 for Outer London and 071 for Inner London.

Entries are current to June 1989.

Index to the Prizes

1	J. R. Ackerley Prize	1
2	Angel Literary Prizes	3
3	Author's Club First Novel Award	5
4	Alice Hunt Bartlett Award	9
5	Bejam Cookery Book of the Year	13
6	James Tait Black Memorial Prizes	14
7	Boardman Tasker Memorial Award for Mountain Literature	32
8	Booker Prize	34
9	British Film Institute Book Award	48
10	Cheltenham Prize	49
11	Arthur C. Clarke Award	51
12	Collins Religious Book Award	52
13	Commonwealth Writers' Prize	54
14	Constable Trophy	55
15	Thomas Cook Travel and Guide Book Awards	56
16	Duff Cooper Memorial Prize	59
17	Crime Writers' Association Awards	65
18	Hunter Davies Prize for the Lakeland Book of the Year	78
19	Mary Elgin Prize	80
20	Geoffrey Faber Memorial Prize	83
21	Fawcett Society Book Prize	88
22	*Guardian* Fiction Prize	90
23	Hawthornden Prize	94
24	David Higham Prize for Fiction	101
25	Historical Novel Prize in Memory of Georgette Heyer	104
26	Winifred Holtby Memorial Prize	106
27	Nelson Hurst and Marsh Biography Award	108
28	Sir Peter Kent Conservation Book Prize	109
29	King George's Fund for Sailors Book of the Sea Award	110

Index to the Prizes

30	London Tourist Board Guide Book of the Year Awards	114
31	Roger Machell Prize	116
32	Mackenzie Prize	117
33	McVitie's Prize for the Scottish Writer of the Year	118
34	Somerset Maugham Award	119
35	MIND Book of the Year	129
36	NCR Book Award for Non-Fiction	131
37	Odd Fellows (Manchester Unity) Social Concern Book Award	133
38	Portico Prize	137
39	John Llewellyn Rhys Memorial Prize	139
40	Romantic Novelists Association Awards	146
41	Royal Society of Literature Award under the W. H. Heinemann Bequest	151
42	Runciman Award	155
43	Saltire Society and *The Scotsman* Literary Award	156
44	Science Book Prize	158
45	Scottish Arts Council Book Awards	159
46	SCSE Book Prizes	171
47	Silver Pen Awards	173
48	André Simon Memorial Fund Book Awards	177
49	W. H. Smith Literary Award	180
50	Southern Arts Literature Prize	185
51	Winifred Mary Stanford Prize	187
52	*Sunday Express* Book of the Year Award	188
53	Betty Trask Awards	190
54	TSB Peninsula Prize	194
55	Welsh Arts Council Awards	195
56	Whitbread Literary Awards	204
57	H. H. Wingate Prize	213
58	*Yorkshire Post* Awards	217

New Prizes

Ian St James Awards	231
P. G. Wodehouse Prize	231

LIST OF PRIZES

1 J. R. Ackerley Prize

Awarded for an autobiography published in the previous year. The winner receives £500.

Contact   English Centre for International PEN
7 Dilke Street
London SW3 4JE
Tel. 01-352 6303

1983

Kathleen Dayus
Her people: Memories of an Edwardian childhood
Chivers Press, 1986. ISBN 0-85119-356-0*
Virago, 1982. (pbk). ISBN 0-86068-275-7*

Ted Walker
The high path
Routledge & Kegan Paul, 1982.
ISBN 0-7100-9302-0*

1984

Richard Charles Cobb
Still life: A Tunbridge Wells childhood
Chatto & Windus, 1983. ISBN 0-7011-2695-7
Hogarth Press, 1985. (pbk). ISBN 0-7012-1920-3*

1985

Angelica Garnett
Deceived with kindness: A Bloomsbury childhood
Chatto & Windus, 1984. ISBN 0-7011-2821-6*
Oxford University Press, 1985. (pbk).
ISBN 0-19-281912-7*

1986

Dan Jacobson
Time and time again: Autobiographies
Deutsch, 1985. ISBN 0-233-97804-6*
Fontana, 1986. (pbk). ISBN 0-00-654184-4*

J. R. Ackerley Prize

1987

Diana Athill
After a funeral
Cape, 1986. ISBN 0-224-02834-0
Hamish Hamilton, 1987. (pbk).
ISBN 0-241-12356-9*

1988

Anthony Burgess
Little Wilson and big God
Heinemann, 1987. ISBN 0-434-09819-1*
Penguin, 1988. (pbk). ISBN 0-14-010824-6*

1989

John Healy
The grass arena: An autobiography
Faber & Faber, 1989. ISBN 0-571-15170-1*

2 Angel Literary Prizes

Two prizes are awarded to authors living and working in East Anglia: £1,000 for a work of fiction and £500 for non-fiction.

Contact The Angel Hotel
Angel Hill
Bury St Edmunds
Suffolk
Tel. (0284) 753926

1984
fiction **Ruth Rendell**
The killing doll
Hutchinson, 1984. ISBN 0-09-155480-2*
Chivers Press, 1985. (large print ed.).
ISBN 0-85119-327-7*
Arrow Books, 1985. (pbk). ISBN 0-09-939950-4*

non-fiction **Norman Lewis**
Voices of the old sea
Hamilton, 1984. ISBN 0-241-11319-9*
Isis Large Print Books, 1985.
ISBN 1-85089-087-0*
Penguin, 1985. (pbk). ISBN 0-14-007780-4*

1985
fiction **Rose Tremain**
The swimming pool season
Hamilton, 1985. ISBN 0-241-11496-9*
Hodder & Stoughton, 1986. (pbk).
ISBN 0-340-39269-X*

non-fiction **Colin Ward and Denis Hardy**
Arcadia for all: The legacy of a makeshift landscape
Mansell, 1984. ISBN 0-7201-1679-1*
Mansell, 1984. (pbk). ISBN 0-7201-1743-7*

1986
fiction **Ronald Blythe**
Stories
Chatto & Windus, 1985. ISBN 0-7011-2965-4

Angel Literary Prizes

non-fiction
Oliver Rackham
History of the countryside: The full fascinating story of Britain's landscape
Dent, 1986. ISBN 0-460-04449-4*
Dent, 1987. (pbk). ISBN 0-460-12552-4*

1987
fiction
Jan Mark
Zeno was here
Cape, 1987. ISBN 0-224-02430-2*

non-fiction
George Macbeth
A child of war
Cape, 1987. ISBN 0-224-02436-1*

1988
fiction
Barbara Vine
The house of stairs
Viking, 1988. ISBN 0-670-82414-3*
Penguin, 1989. (pbk). ISBN 0-14-011446-7*

non-fiction
Ethne Clarke
The art of the kitchen garden
Michael Joseph, 1988. ISBN 0-00-412373-5*

3 Author's Club First Novel Award

A prize of £200 and a silver-mounted quill has been presented for the most promising first novel of the year since 1954. Until 1967 only male writers were eligible.

Contact The Secretary
Author's Club
40 Dover Street
London W1X 3RB
Tel. 01-499 8581

1954

David Unwin
The governor's wife
Michael Joseph, 1964. BNB B54-9849

1955

Brian Moore
The lonely passion of Judith Hearne
Deutsch, 1975. ISBN 0-233-96699-4
Grafton, 1988. (pbk). ISBN 0-586-08758-3*

1956

Harry Bloom
Episode
Collins, 1956. BNB B56-7233

1957

Edmund Ward
Summer in retreat
MacGibbon, 1957. BNB B57-13836

1958

Alan Sillitoe
Saturday night, Sunday morning
W. H. Allen, 1958. ISBN 0-491-00200-9*
Grafton, 1986. (pbk). ISBN 0-586-06502-4*

1959

David Caute
At fever pitch
Deutsch, 1959. BNB B59-01668

Author's Club First Novel Award

1960
> **Lionel Davidson**
> *Night of Wenceslas*
> Gollancz, 1960. BNB B60-00637

1961
> **Jim Hunter**
> *The sun in the morning*
> Faber & Faber, 1961. BNB B61-09547

1962
> **John Pearson**
> *Gone to Timbuctu*
> Collins, 1962. BNB B62-3653

1963
> **David Rubin**
> *The greater darkness*
> Longman, 1963. BNB B63-9536

1964
> **Robin Douglas-Home**
> *Hot for certainties*
> Longman, 1964. BNB B66-8941

1965/6
> **James Mossman**
> *Beggars on horseback*
> Bodley Head, 1965. BNB B66-9687

1967
> **Paul Bailey**
> *At the Jerusalem*
> Cape, 1967. BNB B67-10626
> Penguin, 1982. (pbk). ISBN 0-14-005796-X*

1968
> **Barry England**
> *Figures in a landscape*
> Cape, 1968. ISBN 0-224-61303-0

1969
> **Peter Tinniswood**
> *A touch of Daniel*
> Hodder & Stoughton, 1968. ISBN 0-340-04336-9

Author's Club First Novel Award

1970
    Rachel Ingalls
    Theft
    Faber & Faber, 1970. ISBN 0-571-09477-5*
    Faber & Faber, 1970. (pbk). ISBN 0-571-13991-4*

1971
    Rosemary Hawley Jarman
    We speak no treason
    Collins, 1971. ISBN 0-00-221938-7

1973/4
    Jennifer Johnston
    The captains and the kings
    Hamish Hamilton, 1972. ISBN 0-241-02114-6*
    Fontana, 1985. (pbk). ISBN 0-00-654104-6*

1975/6
    Sasha Moorsom
    A lavender trip
    Bodley Head, 1976. ISBN 0-370-10593-1

1977
    Barbara Benson
    The underlings
    Constable, 1977. ISBN 0-09-461760-0

1978
    Katharine Gordon
    The emerald peacock
    Hodder & Stoughton, 1987. ISBN 0-340-22892-X*
    Ulverscroft Large Print Books, 1979.
    ISBN 0-7089-0329-0*
    Hodder & Stoughton, 1980. (pbk).
    ISBN 0-340-25376-2*

1979
    Martin Page
    The Pilate plot
    Heinemann, 1979. ISBN 0-434-57510-0

1980
    Dawn Lowe-Watson
    The good morrow
    Heinemann, 1980. ISBN 0-434-42945-7
    Magna Print Books, 1982. (large print ed.).
    ISBN 0-86009-370-0*

Author's Club First Novel Award

1981

Anne Smith
The magic glass
Michael Joseph, 1981. ISBN 0-7181-1986-X*

1982

Francis Vernon
Privileged children
Michael Joseph, 1982. ISBN 0-7181-2165-1
Futura, 1985. (pbk). ISBN 0-7088-2842-6*

1983

Katherine Moore
Summer at the haven
Allison & Busby, 1983. ISBN 0-85031-511-5*

1984

Frederick R. Hyde Chambers
Lama: A novel of Tibet
Souvenir Press, 1984. ISBN 0-285-62626-4

1985

Magda Sweetland
Eightsome reel
Macmillan, 1985. ISBN 0-330-24415-9
Pan, 1986. (pbk). ISBN 0-330-29385-0*

1986

Helen Harris
Playing fields in winter
Century, 1986. ISBN 0-7126-9408-0*
Futura, 1987. (pbk). ISBN 0-7088-3370-5*

1987

Peter Benson
The levels
Constable, 1987. ISBN 0-09-467680-1*
Penguin, 1988. (pbk). ISBN 0-14-010635-9*

1988

Gilbert Adair
The holy innocents
Heinemann, 1989. ISBN 0-434-04578-0*

4 Alice Hunt Bartlett Award

An annual award of £500 for a published collection of poetry of no fewer than 20 poems or 400 lines. Special consideration is given to younger or newly emerging poets.

Contact The Poetry Society
21 Earls Court Square
London SW5 9DE
Tel. 01-373 7861

1966

Gavin Bantock
Christ: A poem in 26 parts
Donald Parsons, 1965. BNB B67-17602

Paul Roche
All things considered
Duckworth, 1966. BNB B66-8049

1967

Ted Walker
The solitaires: Poems 1964–5
Cape, 1970. ISBN 0-224-61808-3

1968

Gael Turnbull
A trampoline: Poems 1952–64
Cape Goliard Press, 1968. ISBN 0-206-61556-6

1969

Tom Raworth
The relation ship
Cape Goliard, 1969. ISBN 0-206-61752-6

1970

Leslie Norris
Ransoms
Chatto & Windus, 1970. ISBN 0-7011-1595-5

Alice Hunt Bartlett Award

1971

    Geoffrey Hill
    Mercian hymns
    Deutsch, 1971. (pbk). ISBN 0-233-96794-X*
    Deutsch, 1971. (pbk). ISBN 0-233-96794-X*

1972

    Paul Evans
    February
    Fulcrum Press, 1971

1973

    Rodney Pybus
    In memoriam Milena
    Chatto & Windus, 1973. ISBN 0-7011-1964-0

1974

    Allen Fisher
    Place
    Aloes Books, 1974. ISBN 0-85652-010-1*

    Bill Griffiths
    War with Windsor
    Pirate Press/Writers Forum, 1976.
    ISBN 0-905194-04-7

1975

    Elizabeth Ashworth
    A new confusion
    Outposts Publications, 1975.
    ISBN 0-7205-0405-8

1976

    Lee Harwood
    HMS Little Fox
    Oasis Books, 1975. ISBN 0-903375-22-2*

    Andrew Crozier
    Pleats
    Great Works Editions, 1975. ISBN 0-905383-01-X

1977

    Kit Wright
    The bear looked over the mountain
    Salamander, 1977. ISBN 0-904632-11-3*

Alice Hunt Bartlett Award

1978

John Montague
The great cloak
Dolmen Press, 1978. ISBN 0-85105-327-0*

1979

Simon Lowy
Melusine and the Nigredo
Carcanet Press, 1979. ISBN 0-85635-257-8*

1980

John Whitworth
Unhistorical fragments
Secker & Warburg, 1980. ISBN 0-436-57095-5

1981

Thomas McCarthy
The sorrow garden
Anvil Poetry Press, 1981. ISBN 0-85646-082-6*

Carol Rumens
Unplayed music
Secker & Warburg, 1981. ISBN 0-436-43900-X

1982

Medbh McGuckian
The flower master
Oxford University Press, 1982.
ISBN 0-19-211949-4*

1983

David Constantine
Watching for dolphins
Bloodaxe, 1983. ISBN 0-906427-54-1*

1984

Alison Fell
Kisses for Mayakovsky
Virago, 1984. (pbk). ISBN 0-86068-593-4*

Paul Hyland
The stubborn forest
Bloodaxe, 1984. (pbk). ISBN 0-906427-59-2*

Alice Hunt Bartlett Award

1985

Vikram Seth
The humble administrator's garden
Carcanet Press, 1985. (pbk).
ISBN 0-85635-583-6*

John Davies
The visitor's book
Poetry Wales Press, 1985. (pbk).
ISBN 0-907476-41-4*

1986

Helen Dunmore
The sea skater
Bloodaxe, 1986. (pbk). ISBN 1-85224-006-7*

1987

Sujata Bhatt
Brunizem
Carcanet Press, 1988. (pbk).
ISBN 0-85635-735-9*

5 Bejam Cookery Book of the Year

A prize of £2,500 is awarded for an outstanding new cookery book which is envisaged as 'a collection of original, wholesome food information for family, special occasion, international and health food cookery'. Entries are to have a published price of not more than £20.

Contact Public Relations Department
Bejam
1 Garland Road
Honeypot Lane
Stanmore
Middlesex HA7 1LE

1984

Carol Bowen
Versatile vegetables
Octopus, 1984. ISBN 0-7064-2065-9

1985

Miriam Polunin
The new cookbook
Macdonald, 1985. ISBN 0-356-10550-4*
Macdonald, 1985. (pbk). ISBN 0-356-12351-0*

1986

Nanette Newman
The summer cookbook
Hamlyn, 1986. ISBN 0-600-32607-1*

1987

Antonio Carluccio
An invitation to Italian cooking
Pavilion, 1986. ISBN 1-85145-074-2*
Pan, 1988. (pbk). ISBN 0-330-29922-0*

1988

Christof Buey
Cuisine santé
Sidgwick & Jackson, 1987. ISBN 0-283-99539-4*
Sidgwick & Jackson, 1987. (pbk).
ISBN 0-283-99727-3*

6 James Tait Black Memorial Prizes

Two of the oldest prizes in the UK. Two prizes, of £1,000 each, are awarded each year for the best fiction and biography published in the previous year.

Contact   Department of English Literature
University of Edinburgh
George Square
Edinburgh EH8 9JX

1919
fiction

Hugh Walpole
The secret city: A novel in three parts
Macmillan, 1919

biography

Henry Festing Jones
Samuel Butler: Author of Erewhon: 1835–1902, a memoir
Macmillan, 1919

1920
fiction

D. H. Lawrence
The lost girl
Heinemann, 1920
Penguin, 1970. (pbk). ISBN 0-14-000752-0*

biography

G. M. Trevelyan
Lord Grey of the Reform Bill
Greenwood Press, new ed. 1970
ISBN 0-8371-4553-8*

1921
fiction

Walter de la Mare
Memoirs of a midget
Collins, 1921
Oxford University Press, 1982. (pbk).
ISBN 0-19-281344-7*

James Tait Black Memorial Prizes

biography	**Lytton Strachey** *Queen Victoria* Chatto & Windus, 1921 Penguin, 1971. (pbk). ISBN 0-14-003241-X*
1922 fiction	**David Garnett** *Lady into fox* Chatto & Windus, 1922 Hogarth Press, 1985. (pbk). ISBN 0-7012-1923-8*
biography	**Percy Lubbock** *Earlham* Greenwood Press, new ed. 1974. ISBN 0-8371-7722-7*
1923 fiction	**Arnold Bennett** *Riceyman Steps* Cassell, 1923 Oxford University Press, 1983. (pbk). ISBN 0-19-281373-0*
biography	**Ronald Ross** *Memoirs: With a full account of the great malaria problem and its solution* John Murray, 1923
1924 fiction	**E. M. Forster** *A passage to India* Edward Arnold, 1924 Ulverscroft Large Print Books, 1981. ISBN 0-7089-8000-7* Macmillan, 1987. (pbk). ISBN 0-333-43341-6* Penguin, 1985. (pbk). ISBN 0-14-006527-X*
biography	**William Wilson** *The house of Airlie* John Murray, 1924
1925 fiction	**Liam O'Flaherty** *The informer* Cape, 1925

James Tait Black Memorial Prizes

biography
Geoffrey Scott
Portrait of Zelide
Constable, 1925

1926
fiction
Radycliffe Hall
Adam's breed
Cassell, 1926
Virago, 1985. (pbk). ISBN 0-86068-617-5*

biography
H. B. Workman
John Wyclif: A study of the English medieval church
Clarendon Press, 1926

1927
fiction
Francis Brett Young
Portrait of Clare
Heinemann, 1927
Chivers Press, 1973. (large print ed.).
ISBN 0-85594-846-9

biography
H. A. L. Fisher
James Bryce
Greenwood Press, new ed. 1973.
ISBN 0-8371-4797-2*

1928
fiction
Siegfried Sassoon
Memoirs of a fox-hunting man
Faber & Faber, 1928
Faber & Faber, 1980. (pbk).
ISBN 0-571-06454-X*

biography
John Buchan
Montrose: A history
Greenwood Press, new ed. 1975.
ISBN 0-8371-7795-2*

1929
fiction
J. B. Priestley
The good companions
Heinemann, 1929
Panther, 1981. (pbk). ISBN 0-434-60307-4*

James Tait Black Memorial Prizes

biography
Lord David Cecil
The stricken deer: William Cowper
Constable, 1988. (pbk). ISBN 0-09-468430-8*

1930
fiction
E. H. Young
Miss Mole
Cape, 1930
Virago, 1984. (pbk). ISBN 0-86068-431-8*

biography
Francis Yeats Brown
Bengal lancer
Gollancz, 1930
A. Mott, 1984. (pbk). ISBN 0-907746-35-7*

1931
fiction
Kate O'Brien
Without my cloak
Heinemann, 1931
Virago, 1986. (pbk). ISBN 0-86068-760-0*

biography
J. Y. T. Greig
David Hume
Cape, 1931

1932
fiction
Helen Simpson
Boomerang
Heinemann, 1932

biography
Stephen Gwynn
The life of Mary Kingsley
Macmillan, 1932

1933
fiction
A. G. Macdonell
England, their England
Macmillan, 1933. ISBN 0-333-02425-7*
Pan, 1983. (pbk). ISBN 0-330-28041-4*

biography
Violet Clifton
The book of the Talbot: A life of John Talbot
Faber & Faber, 1933

1934
fiction   **Robert Graves**
           I, Claudius
           Methuen, 1976. ISBN 0-413-37070-4*
           Penguin, 1969. (pbk). ISBN 0-14-000318-5*

           Claudius the God
           Methuen, 1976. ISBN 0-413-37080-1*
           Penguin, 1970. (pbk). ISBN 0-14-000421-1*
           Penguin, 1986. ISBN 0-14-009314-1

biography **J. E. Neale**
           Queen Elizabeth
           Cape, 1934
           Panther, 1979. (pbk). ISBN 0-586-04973-8

1935
fiction   **L. H. Myers**
           The root and the flower
           Cape, 1935
           Oxford University Press, 1985. (pbk).
           ISBN 0-19-281911-9*

biography **R. W. Chambers**
           Thomas More
           Cape, 1935
           Harvester Press, 1982. (pbk).
           ISBN 0-7108-0337-0*

1936
fiction   **Winifred Holtby**
           South Riding
           Collins, new ed. 1966. ISBN 0-00-221761-9*
           Fontana, 1974. (pbk). ISBN 0-00-613654-0*

biography **Edward Sackville-West**
           A flame in sunlight: The life and work of Thomas de Quincey
           Cassell, 1936

1937
fiction   **Neil M. Gunn**
           Highland river
           Porpoise Press, 1937
           Arrow, 1974. (pbk). ISBN 0-09-908720-0*

James Tait Black Memorial Prizes

biography **Lord Eustace Percy**
John Knox
John Clarke, 1964. ISBN 0-227-67510-X*

1938
fiction **C. S. Forester**
A ship of the line and *Flying colours*
Michael Joseph, 1938
Penguin, 1969. (pbk). ISBN 0-14-001114-5*

biography **Sir Edmund Chambers**
Samuel Taylor Coleridge
Clarendon Press, 1938

1939
fiction **Aldous Huxley**
After many a summer
Chatto & Windus, 1939
Panther, 1976. (pbk). ISBN 0-586-04432-9*

biography **David C. Douglas**
English scholars: 1660–1730
Greenwood Press, new ed. 1976.
ISBN 0-8371-8093-7*

1940
fiction **Charles Morgan**
The voyage
Macmillan, 1940

biography **Hilda F. M. Prescott**
A Spanish Tudor: The life of Bloody Mary
Constable, 1940

1941
fiction **Joyce Cary**
A house of children
Michael Joseph, 1941

biography **John Gore**
King George V
John Murray, 1949

1942
fiction   **Arthur Waley**
Monkey (translated from) Wu Ch'eng-en
John Day, 1942
Unwin, 1984. (pbk). ISBN 0-04-823276-9*

biography   **Lord Ponsonby of Shulbrede**
Henry Ponsonby: Queen Victoria's private secretary
Macmillan, 1942

1943
fiction   **Mary Lavin**
Tales from Bectine Bridge
Michael Joseph, 1943

biography   **G. G. Coulton**
Fourscore years: An autobiography
Cambridge University Press, 1943

1944
fiction   **Forrest Reid**
Young Tom, or, very mixed company
Faber & Faber, 1944
GMP Publishers, 1987. ISBN 0-85449-055-8*

biography   **C. V. Wedgewood**
William the Silent: William of Nassau, Prince of Orange
Cape, 1944

1945
fiction   **L. A. G. Strong**
Travellers
Methuen, 1945

biography   **D. S. Maccoll**
Life, work and setting of Philip Wilson Steer
Faber & Faber, 1945

1946
fiction   **G. Oliver Onions**
Poor man's tapestry
Michael Joseph, 1946

James Tait Black Memorial Prizes

biography   **R. Aldington**
The Duke: Being an account of the life and achievements of Arthur Wellesley, 1st Duke of Wellington
Viking Press, 1943

1947
fiction   **L. P. Hartley**
Eustace and Hilda: A trilogy
Putnam, new ed. 1958. ISBN 0-370-00039-0*
Faber & Faber, 1979. (pbk). ISBN 0-571-11402-4*

biography   **C. E. Raven**
English naturalists: From Neckham to Ray
Cambridge University Press, 1947

1948
fiction   **Graham Greene**
The heart of the matter
Bodley Head, new ed. 1971.
ISBN 0-370-01443-X*
Heinemann, new ed. 1971. ISBN 0-434-30557-X*
Penguin, 1969. (pbk). ISBN 0-14-001896-4*

biography   **Percy A. Scholes**
The great Doctor Burney: His life, his travels, his works, his family, his friends
Greenwood Press, new ed. 1971
ISBN 0-8371-4017-X*

1949
fiction   **Emma Smith**
The far cry
MacGibbon & Kee, 1949
Penguin, 1952. (pbk). BNB B52-06584

biography   **John Connell**
W. E. Henley
Constable, 1949

1950
fiction   **Robert Henriquez**
Through the valley
Collins, 1950. BNB B50-5848

biography	**Cecil Woodham-Smith** *Florence Nightingale: 1820–1910* Constable, 1950. BNB B50-08794
1951 fiction	**Chapman Mortimer** *Father Goose* Hart-Davis, 1951. BNB B51-2993
biography	**Noel G. Annan** *Leslie Stephen: The Godless Victorian* Weidenfeld & Nicolson, new ed. 1984. ISBN 0-297-78369-6* University of Chicago Press, 1986. (pbk). ISBN 0-226-02106-8*
1952 fiction	**Evelyn Waugh** *Men at arms* Chapman & Hall, 1952. BNB B52-11847
biography	**G. M. Young** *Stanley Baldwin* Greenwood Press, new ed. 1979. ISBN 0-313-21041-1
1953 fiction	**Margaret Kennedy** *Troy chimneys* Macmillan, 1953. BNB B53-01284 Virago, 1985. (pbk). ISBN 0-86068-566-7*
biography	**Carola Oman** *Sir John Moore* Hodder & Stoughton, 1953. BNB B53-14279
1954 fiction	**C. P. Snow** *The new men* Macmillan, 1954. BNB B54-05514 Penguin, 1970. (pbk). ISBN 0-14-001356-3* *The masters* Macmillan, 1951. BNB B51-08378 Penguin, 1969. (pbk). ISBN 0-14-001089-0*

James Tait Black Memorial Prizes

biography   **Keith Feiling**
Warren Hastings
Macmillan, 1954. BNB B54-08118

1955
fiction   **Ivy Compton-Burnett**
Mother and son
Gollancz, 1955. BNB B55-01689

biography   **R. W. Ketton-Cremer**
Thomas Gray
Longman, 1955. BNB B58-18962

1956
fiction   **Rose Macaulay**
The towers of Trebizond
Collins, 1965. ISBN 0-00-221804-6*
Futura, 1981. (pbk). ISBN 0-7088-2081-6*

biography   **St John Greer Ervine**
George Bernard Shaw: His life, work and friends
Constable, new ed. 1972. ISBN 0-09-458630-6*

1957
fiction   **Anthony Powell**
At Lady Molly's
Heinemann, 1957. ISBN 0-434-59903-4*

biography   **Maurice Cranston**
Life of John Locke
Longman, 1957. ISBN 0-582-11215-X*
Longman, 1970. (pbk). ISBN 0-582-01135-3*

1958
fiction   **Angus Wilson**
The middle age of Mrs Eliot
Secker & Warburg, 1958. ISBN 0-436-57505-1*

biography   **Joyce Hemlow**
The history of Fanny Burney
Oxford University Press, 1958.
ISBN 0-19-811549-0*

James Tait Black Memorial Prizes

1959
fiction

Morris West
The Devil's advocate
Heinemann, 1959. BNB 59-13893
Ulverscroft Large Print, 1974.
ISBN 0-85456-274-5*
Fontana, 1977. (pbk). ISBN 0-00-614460-8*

biography

Christopher Hassall
Edward Marsh: Patron of the arts
Longman, 1959. BNB B59-9061

1960
fiction

Rex Warner
Imperial Caesar
Collins, 1960. BNB B60-14190

biography

Adam Fox
The life of Dean Inge
John Murray, 1960. BNB B64-11616

1961
fiction

Jennifer Dawson
The ha-ha
Blond, 1961. BNB B61-01207
Virago, 1985. (pbk). ISBN 0-86068-575-6*

biography

M. K. Ashby
Joseph Ashby of Tysoe: 1859–1919
Merlin Press, 2nd ed. 1974.
ISBN 0-85036-174-5*
Merlin Press, 2nd ed. 1974. (pbk).
ISBN 0-85036-180-X*

1962
fiction

Ronald Hardy
Act of destruction
Weidenfeld & Nicolson, 1962. BNB B62-10568

biography

Meriol Trevor
Newman: The pillar and the cloud
Macmillan, 1962. BNB B62-3173

Newman: Light in winter
Macmillan, 1962. BNB B62-16492

1963
fiction

Gerda Charles
A slanting light
Eyre, 1963. BNB B63-7290

biography

Georgina Battiscome
John Keble: A study in limitations
Constable, 1963. BNB B63-19265

1964
fiction

Frank Tuohy
The ice saints
Macmillan, 1964. BNB B64-11998

biography

Elizabeth Longford
Victoria RI
Weidenfeld & Nicolson, 1964
BNB B64-17758
Weidenfeld & Nicolson, 1988. (pbk).
ISBN 0-297-79377-3*

1965
fiction

Muriel Spark
The Mandelbaum gate
Macmillan, 1965. ISBN 0-333-04142-9*
Penguin, 1970. (pbk). ISBN 0-14-002745-9*

biography

Mary Moorman
William Wordsworth: The later years 1803–1850
Oxford University Press, 1965. BNB B65-19832

1966
fiction

Christine Brooke-Rose
Such
Michael Joseph, 1966. BNB B66-19578

Aidan Higgins
Langrishe, go down
Calder & Boyars, 1966. BNB B66-01650
Grafton, 1987. (pbk). ISBN 0-586-08566-1*

James Tait Black Memorial Prizes

biography   **Geoffrey Keynes**
The life of William Harvey
Oxford University Press, 1966.
ISBN 0-19-858119-X*

1967
fiction   **Margaret Drabble**
Jerusalem the golden
Weidenfeld & Nicolson, 1967.
ISBN 0-297-74810-6*
Penguin, 1969. (pbk). ISBN 0-14-002933-8*

biography   **Winifred Gerin**
The life of William Harvey
Oxford University Press, 1966.
ISBN 0-19-858119-X*

1968
fiction   **Maggie Ross**
The gasteropod
Barrie & Rockcliffe, 1968. ISBN 0-214-66690-5
Penguin, 1970. (pbk). ISBN 0-14-005648-3

biography   **Gordon S. Haight**
George Eliot: A biography
Clarendon Press, 1968. ISBN 0-19-811666-7
Penguin, 1986. (pbk). ISBN 0-14-058025-5*

1969
fiction   **Elizabeth Bowen**
Eva Trout
Cape, 1969. ISBN 0-224-61469-X
Penguin, 1982. (pbk). ISBN 0-14-008542-4*

biography   **Lady Antonia Fraser**
Mary, Queen of Scots
Weidenfeld & Nicolson, 1969.
ISBN 0-297-17773-7*
Methuen, 1985. (pbk). ISBN-413-57380-X*

1970
fiction   **Lily Powell**
The bird of paradise
Bodley Head, 1970. ISBN 0-370-01429-4

James Tait Black Memorial Prizes

biography	**Jasper Ridley** *Lord Palmerston* Constable, 1970. ISBN 0-586-03722-5
1971 fiction	**Nadine Gordimer** *A guest of honour* Cape, 1971. ISBN 0-224-00510-3 Penguin, 1973. (pbk). ISBN 0-14-003696-2*
biography	**Julia Namier** *Lewis Namier* Oxford University Press, 1971. ISBN 0-19-211706-8
1972 fiction	**John Berger** *G.* Weidenfeld & Nicolson, 1972. ISBN 0-297-99423-9 Hogarth Press, 1989. (pbk). ISBN 0-7012-0833-3*
biography	**Quentin Bell** *Virginia Woolf* Vol.1 Hogarth Press, 1972. ISBN 0-7012-0291-2 Vol.2 Hogarth Press, 1972. ISBN 0-7012-0371-4 Grafton, 1987. (pbk). ISBN 0-586-08676-5*
1973 fiction	**Iris Murdoch** *The Black Prince* Chatto & Windus, new ed. 1984. ISBN 0-7011-2768-6* Penguin, 1975 (BBIP). (pbk). ISBN 0-14-003934-1*
biography	**Robin Lane-Fox** *Alexander the Great* Allen Lane, 1973. ISBN 0-7139-0500-X Penguin, 1986. (pbk). ISBN 0-14-008878-4*
1974 fiction	**Lawrence Durrell** *Monsieur, or, the Prince of Darkness* Faber & Faber, 1974. ISBN 0-571-10660-9* Faber & Faber, 1974. (pbk). ISBN 0-571-10965-9*

James Tait Black Memorial Prizes

biography
    John Wain
    Samuel Johnson
    Macmillan, 2nd ed. 1980. ISBN 0-333-28543-3*

1975
fiction
    Brian Moore
    The great Victorian collection
    Cape, 1975. ISBN 0-224-01126-X*
    Grafton, 1988. (pbk). ISBN 0-224-01126-X*

biography
    Karl Miller
    Cockburn's millenium
    Duckworth, 1975. ISBN 0-7156-0913-0*
    Duckworth, 1978. (pbk). ISBN 0-7156-1216-6*

1976
fiction
    John Banville
    Doctor Copernicus
    Secker & Warburg, 1976. ISBN 0-436-03263-5*
    Paladin, 1987. (pbk). ISBN 0-586-08414-2*

biography
    Ronald Hingley
    A new life of Chekhov
    Oxford University Press, 1976.
    ISBN 0-19-211729-7

1977
fiction
    John le Carré
    The honourable schoolboy
    Hodder & Stoughton, 1977.
    ISBN 0-340-22042-2*
    Chivers Press, 1987. (large print ed.).
    ISBN 0-86220-222-1*
    G. K. Hall, 1978. (large print ed.).
    ISBN 0-8161-6539-4*
    Pan, 1979. (pbk). ISBN 0-330-25356-5*

biography
    George Painter
    Chateaubriand: A biography. Vol. 1: The longed-for tempests
    Chatto & Windus, 1977. ISBN 0-7011-2184-X

James Tait Black Memorial Prizes

1978
fiction

Maurice Gee
Plumb
Faber & Faber, 1978. ISBN 0-571-11279-X

biography

Robert Gittings
The older Hardy
Heinemann, 1978. ISBN 0-435-18364-8
Penguin, 1980. (pbk). ISBN 0-14-005049-3*

1979
fiction

William Golding
Darkness visible
Faber & Faber, 1979. ISBN 0-571-11454-7*
Faber & Faber, 1981. (pbk). ISBN 0-571-11646-9*

biography

Brian Finney
Christopher Isherwood: A critical biography
Faber & Faber, 1979. ISBN 0-571-11345-1

1980
fiction

J. M. Coetzee
Waiting for the barbarians
Secker & Warburg, 1980. ISBN 0-436-10295-1*
Penguin, 1982. (pbk). ISBN 0-14-006555-5*

biography

Robert Bernard Martin
Tennyson: The unquiet heart
Oxford University Press, 1980.
ISBN 0-19-812072-9*
Faber & Faber, 1983. (pbk). ISBN 0-571-11842-9*

1981
fiction

Salman Rushdie
Midnight's children
Cape, 1981. ISBN 0-224-01823-X*
Pan, 1984. (pbk). ISBN 0-330-26714-0*

Paul Theroux
The Mosquito Coast
Hamish Hamilton, 1981. ISBN 0-241-10688-5*

James Tait Black Memorial Prizes

biography   **Victoria Glendinning**
Edith Sitwell: Unicorn among lions
Weidenfeld & Nicolson, 1981.
ISBN 0-297-77801-3
Oxford University Press, 1983. (pbk).
ISBN 0-19-281369-2*

1982
fiction   **Bruce Chatwin**
On the black hill
Cape, 1982. ISBN 0-224-01980-5*
Pan, 1983. (pbk). ISBN 0-330-28124-0*

biography   **Richard Ellman**
James Joyce
2nd ed. Oxford University Press, 1982.
ISBN 0-19-503103-2*
2nd ed. Oxford University Press, 1984. (pbk).
ISBN 0-19-503381-7*

1983
fiction   **Jonathan Keates**
Allegro postillions
Salamander, 1983. ISBN 0-907540-36-8*

biography   **Alan Walker**
Franz Liszt: The virtuoso years
Faber & Faber, 1983. ISBN 0-571-10568-8*

1984
fiction   **J. G. Ballard**
Empire of the sun
Gollancz, 1984. ISBN 0-575-03483-1*
Ulverscroft Large Print Books, 1985.
ISBN 0-7089-8270-0*
Granada, 1985. (pbk). ISBN 0-586-06430-3*

Angela Carter
Nights at the circus
Chatto & Windus, 1984. ISBN 0-7011-3932-3*
Pan, 1985. (pbk). ISBN 0-330-28836-9*

James Tait Black Memorial Prizes

biography	**Lyndall Gordon** *Virginia Woolf: A writer's life* Oxford University Press, 1984. ISBN 0-19-811723-X* Oxford University Press, 1986. (pbk). ISBN 0-19-281907-0*
1985 fiction	**Robert Edric** *Winter garden* Deutsch, 1985. ISBN 0-233-97756-2*
biography	**David Noakes** *Jonathan Swift: A hypocrite reversed* Oxford University Press, 1985. ISBN 0-19-812834-7* Oxford University Press, 1987. (pbk). ISBN 0-19-282055-9*
1986 fiction	**Jenny Joseph** *Persephone* Bloodaxe, 1985. ISBN 0-906427-77-0* Bloodaxe, 1985. (pbk). ISBN 0-906427-78-9*
biography	**Felicitas Corrigan** *Helen Waddell* Gollancz, 1986. ISBN 0-575-03674-5*
1987 fiction	**George Mackay Brown** *The golden bird: Two Orkney stories* John Murray, 1987. ISBN 0-7195-4385-1*
biography	**Ruth Dudley Edwards** *Victor Gollancz: A biography* Gollancz, 1987. ISBN 0-575-03175-1*

7 Boardman Tasker Memorial Award for Mountain Literature

The award of £1,000, which commemorates the lives of Peter Boardman and Joe Tasker who were lost on Everest in 1982, is given to the author(s) of a work which has made an outstanding contribution to mountain literature.

Contact Boardman Tasker Award
56 St Michael's Avenue
Bramhall
Stockport
Cheshire SK7 2PL
Tel. (061) 439 4624

1984

Linda Gill
Living high
Hodder & Stoughton, 1984. ISBN 0-340-34815-1

Doug Scott and Alex Macintyre
The Shishapangma expedition
Granada, 1984. ISBN 0-246-12013-4*

1985

Jim Perrin
Menlove
Gollancz, 1985. ISBN 0-575-03571-4

1986

Stephen Venables
Painted mountains: Two expeditions to Kashmir
Hodder & Stoughton, 1986.
ISBN 0-340-39608-3*

1987

Roger Mear and Robert Swan
In the footsteps of Scott
Cape, 1987. ISBN 0-224-02418-3*

Boardman Tasker Memorial Award

1988

Joe Simpson
Touching the void
Cape, 1988. ISBN 0-224-02545-7*
Pan, 1989. (pbk). ISBN 0-330-30859-9*

8 Booker Prize

The Booker is probably Britain's best known literary award. Unlike most other awards the shortlist is published before the winning title is chosen. A great deal of publicity is generated ensuring that a place on the list enhances an author's reputation and increases sales. It is not surprising therefore that the choice of winners, shortlisted titles and judges is often controversial and hot debates in the press ensue that question the value and purpose of awards. The Booker was founded to reward merit and to raise the stature of the author in the eyes of the public. The prize now stands at £15,000.

Contact   Book Trust
                 Book House
                 45 East Hill
                 London SW18 2QZ
                 Tel. 01-870 9055

As the shortlisted titles are almost as important as the winner they have been listed as well.

1969

P.H. Newby
Something to answer for
Faber & Faber, 1968. BNB B68-22011

shortlist   **Barry England**
               Figures in a landscape
               Cape, 1968. ISBN 0-224-61303-0

               Nicholas Mosley
               The impossible object
               Hodder & Stoughton, 1968. ISBN 0-340-04448-9

               Iris Murdoch
               The nice and the good
               Chatto & Windus, 1968. ISBN 0-7011-1261-1*

               Muriel Spark
               The public image
               Macmillan, 1968. ISBN 0-333-09018-7*
               Penguin, 1970. (pbk). ISBN 0-14-003131-6*

G. M. Williams
From scenes like these
Mayflower, 1969. ISBN 0-583-11666-3
Magna Print Books, 1986. (large print ed.)
ISBN 1-85057-022-1*

1970

Bernice Rubens
The elected member
Hamish Hamilton, new ed. 1983.
ISBN 0-241-11112-9*
Sphere, 1986. (pbk). ISBN 0-349-13022-1*

shortlist

A. L. Barker
John Brown's body
Hogarth Press, 1969. ISBN 0-7012-0327-7

Elizabeth Bowen
Eva Trout
Cape, 1969. ISBN 0-224-61469-X
Penguin, 1982. (pbk). ISBN 0-370-01429-4

Iris Murdoch
Bruno's dream
Chatto & Windus, 1969. ISBN 0-7011-1426-6*
Penguin, 1977. (pbk). ISBN 0-14-003176-6*

William Trevor
Mrs Eckdorf in O'Neill's hotel
Bodley Head, 1969. ISBN 0-370-01421-9*
Penguin, 1982. (pbk). ISBN 0-14-006014-6*

T. Wheeler
The conjunction
Angus & Robertson, 1969. ISBN 0-207-95045-8*

1971

V. S. Naipaul
In a free state
Deutsch, 1971. ISBN 0-233-95832-0
Penguin, 1973. (pbk). ISBN 0-14-003711-X*

shortlist

Thomas Kilroy
The big chapel
Faber & Faber, 1971. ISBN 0-571-09700-6

Doris Lessing
Briefing for a descent into hell
Cape, 1971. ISBN 0-586-03817-5
Panther, 1973. (pbk). ISBN 0-586-03817-5*

Mordecai Richler
St Urbain's horseman
Weidenfeld & Nicolson, 1971.
ISBN 0-297-00363-1

Elizabeth Taylor
Mrs Palfrey at the Claremont
Chatto & Windus, 1971. ISBN 0-7011-1782-6
Virago, 1982. (pbk). ISBN 0-86068-263-3*

1972

John Berger
G.
Weidenfeld & Nicolson, 1972.
ISBN 0-297-99423-9
Hogarth Press, 1989. (pbk). ISBN 0-7012-0833-3*

shortlist

Susan Hill
Bird of night
Hamish Hamilton, 1972. ISBN 0-241-02258-4
Penguin, 1976. (pbk). ISBN 0-14-004072-2*

Thomas Keneally
The chant of Jimmy Blacksmith
Angus & Robertson, 1972. ISBN 0-207-12375-6
Fontana, 1984. (pbk). ISBN 0-00-654093-7*

David Storey
Pasmore
Cape, new ed. 1986. ISBN 0-224-02840-5*

1973

J. G. Farrell
The siege of Krishnapur
Weidenfeld & Nicolson, 1973.
ISBN 0-297-76580-9*
Fontana, 1985. (pbk). ISBN 0-00-654117-8*

shortlist   **Beryl Bainbridge**
The dressmaker
Duckworth, 1973. ISBN 0-7156-0721-9*
Fontana, 1985. (pbk). ISBN 0-00-654081-3*

Nadine Gordimer
The conservationist
Cape, 1974. ISBN 0-224-01035-2*
Penguin, 1978. (pbk). ISBN 0-14-004716-6*

Elizabeth Mavor
The green equinox
Wildwood House, 1973. ISBN 0-7045-0046-9

Iris Murdoch
The Black Prince
Chatto & Windus, new ed. 1984.
ISBN 0-7011-2768-6*
Penguin, 1975. (pbk). ISBN 0-14-003934-1*

1974

Stanley Middleton
Holiday
Hutchinson, 1974. ISBN 0-09-119910-7
Arrow, 1988. (pbk). ISBN 0-09-958430-1

shortlist   **Kingsley Amis**
Ending up
Cape, 1974. ISBN 0-224-00988-5*
Penguin, 1987. (pbk). ISBN 0-14-004151-6*

Beryl Bainbridge
The bottle factory outing
Duckworth, 1974. ISBN 0-7156-0864-9*
Fontana, 1985. (pbk). ISBN 0-00-654100-3*

C. P. Snow
In their wisdom
Macmillan, 1974. ISBN 0-333-17365-1

1975

Ruth Prawer Jhabvala
Heat and dust
John Murray, 1975. ISBN 0-7195-3401-1*
Futura, 1976. (pbk). ISBN 0-86007-414-5*

Booker Prize

shortlist
Thomas Keneally
Gossip from the forest
Collins, 1975. ISBN 0-00-222241-8
Hodder & Stoughton, 1984. (pbk).
ISBN 0-340-35474-7*

1976

David Storey
Saville
Cape, 1976. ISBN 0-224-01273-8
Penguin, 1978. (pbk). ISBN 0-14-004611-9*

shortlist
André Brink
An instant in the wind
W. H. Allen, 1976. ISBN 0-491-01617-4*
Fontana, 1983. (pbk). ISBN 0-00-654012-0*

R. C. Hutchinson
Rising
Michael Joseph, 1976. ISBN 0-7181-1523-6

Brian Moore
The doctor's wife
Cape, 1976. ISBN 0-224-01322-X*
Grafton, 1988. ISBN 0-586-08739-7*

Julian Rathbone
King fisher lives
Michael Joseph, 1976. ISBN 0-7181-1471-X

William Trevor
The children of Dynmouth
Bodley Head, 1976. ISBN 0-370-10561-3*
Penguin 1979. (pbk). ISBN 0-14-004718-2*
Penguin, 1982. (pbk). ISBN 0-14-006263-7*

1977

Paul Scott
Staying on
Heinemann, 1977. ISBN 0-434-68113-X*
Longman, 1985. (pbk). ISBN 0-582-35438-2*
Panther, 1978. (pbk). ISBN 0-586-04585-6*

shortlist
Paul Bailey
Peter Smart's confessions
Cape, 1977. ISBN 0-224-01358-0*

Caroline Blackwood
Great Granny Webster
Duckworth, 1977. ISBN 0-224-01358-0*

Jennifer Johnston
Shadows on our skin
Hamish Hamilton, 1977. ISBN 0-241-89661-4*
Fontana, 1986. (pbk). ISBN 0-00-654131-3*
Heinemann Educational, 1987. (pbk).
ISBN 0-435-12317-3*

Penelope Lively
The road to Lichfield
Heinemann, 1977. ISBN 0-434-42735-7
Chivers Press, 1980. (large print ed.).
ISBN 0-7451-7017-X*
Penguin, 1983. (pbk). ISBN 0-14-006117-7*

Barbara Pym
Quartet in Autumn
Macmillan, 1977. ISBN 0-333-22778-6*
Panther, 1980. (pbk). ISBN 0-586-05033-7*

1978

Iris Murdoch
The sea, the sea
Chatto & Windus, new ed. 1984.
ISBN 0-7011-2838-0*
Panther, 1980. (pbk). ISBN 0-586-04976-2*

shortlist

Kingsley Amis
Jake's thing
Hutchinson, 1978. ISBN 0-09-134390-9*
Penguin, 1980. (pbk). ISBN 0-14-005096-5*

André Brink
Rumours of rain
W.H. Allen, 1978. ISBN 0-491-02005-8*
Fontana, 1984. (pbk). ISBN 0-00-654013-9*
Star, 1979. (pbk). ISBN 0-352-30591-6*

Penelope Fitzgerald
The bookshop
Duckworth, 1978. ISBN 0-7156-1320-0

Jane Gardam
God on the rocks
Hamish Hamilton, 1978. ISBN 0-241-10061-5*
Sphere, 1981. (pbk). ISBN 0-349-11406-4

Bernice Rubens
A five year sentence
Hamish Hamilton, 1983. ISBN 0-2411139-0*
Sphere, 1988. (pbk). ISBN 0-349-13021-3*

1979

Penelope Fitzgerald
Offshore
Collins, 1979. ISBN 0-00-221614-0
Fontana, 1988. (pbk.) ISBN 0-00-654256-5*

shortlist

Thomas Keneally
Confederates
Collins, 1979. ISBN 0-00-222141-1*

V. S. Naipaul
A bend in the river
Deutsch, 1979. ISBN 0-233-97140-8*
Penguin, 1980. (pbk). ISBN 0-14-005258-5*

Julian Rathbone
Joseph
Michael Joseph, 1979. ISBN 0-7181-1704-2

Fay Weldon
Praxis
Hodder & Stoughton, 1979.
ISBN 0-340-23295-1*
Hodder & Stoughton, 1980. (pbk).
ISBN 0-340-25375-4*

1980

William Golding
Rites of passage
Faber & Faber, 1980. ISBN 0-571-11639-6*
Faber & Faber, 1982. (pbk).
ISBN 0-571-08988-7*

shortlist **Anthony Burgess**
Earthly powers
Hutchinson, 1980. ISBN 0-09-143910-8
Penguin, 1981. (pbk). ISBN 0-14-005896-6*

Anita Desai
Clear light of day
Heinemann, 1980. ISBN 0-434-18633-3*
Penguin, 1986. (pbk). ISBN 0-14-00-8670-6*

Alice Munro
The beggar maid
Allen Lane, 1980. ISBN 0-7139-1317-7
Penguin, 1981. (pbk). ISBN 0-14-006011-1*

Julia O'Faolain
No country for young men
Allen Lane, 1980. ISBN 0-7181-1854-5

Barry Unsworth
Pascali's island
Michael Joseph, 1980. ISBN 0-7181-1854-5

J. L. Carr
A month in the country
Harvester Press, 1980. ISBN 0-85527-328-3*
Isis Large Print Books, 1988.
ISBN 0-85089-253-9*

1981

Salman Rushdie
Midnight's children
Cape, 1981. ISBN 0-224-01823-X*
Pan, 1982. (pbk). ISBN 0-330-26714-0*

shortlist **Molly Keane**
Good behaviour
Deutsch, 1981. ISBN 0-233-97332-X
Sphere, 1982. (pbk). ISBN 0-349-12075-7

Doris Lessing
The Sirian experiments
Cape, 1981. ISBN 0-224-01891-4*
Granada, 1982. (pbk). ISBN 0-586-05475-8*

Ian McEwan
The comfort of strangers
Cape, 1981. ISBN 0-224-01931-7*
Pan, 1982. (pbk). ISBN 0-330-26829-5*

Anne Schlee
Rhine journey
Penguin, 1981. (pbk). ISBN 0-14-006215-7*

Muriel Spark
Loitering with intent
Bodley Head, 1981. ISBN 0-370-30900-6*
Granada, 1982. (pbk). ISBN 0-586-05584-3*

D. M. Thomas
The White Hotel
Gollancz, 1981. ISBN 0-575-02889-0*
Penguin, 1988. (pbk). ISBN 0-14-010803-3*

1982

Thomas Keneally
Schindler's ark
Hodder & Stoughton, 1982. ISBN 0-340-27838-2
Chivers Press, 1985. (large print ed.).
ISBN 0-86220-122-5*
Hodder & Stoughton, 1983. (pbk).
ISBN 0-340-33501-7*

shortlist
John Arden
Silence among the weapons
Methuen, 1982. ISBN 0-413-49670-8*
Methuen, 1983. (pbk). ISBN 0-413-52310-1*

William Boyd
An ice cream war
Hamish Hamilton, 1982. ISBN 0-241-10868-3
Penguin, 1983. (pbk). ISBN 0-14-006571-7*

Lawrence Durrell
Constance, or, solitary practices
Faber & Faber, 1982. ISBN 0-571-11757-0*
Faber & Faber, 1983. (pbk).
ISBN 0-571-13102-6*

1983

Alice Thomas Ellis
The 27th kingdom
Duckworth, 1982. ISBN 0-7156-1645-5*
Penguin, 1982. (pbk). ISBN 0-14-006704-3*

Timothy Mo
Sour sweet
Deutsch, 1982. ISBN 0-233-97365-6*
Sphere, 1983. (pbk). ISBN 0-349-12392-6*

J. M. Coetzee
Life and times of Michael K
Secker & Warburg, 1983. ISBN 0-436-10297-8*
Penguin, 1985. (pbk). ISBN 0-14-007115-6*

shortlist

Malcolm Bradbury
Rates of exchange
Secker & Warburg, 1983. ISBN 0-436-06505-3*
Arrow, 1984. (pbk). ISBN 0-09-934000-3*

John Fuller
Flying to nowhere
Salamander Press, 1983. ISBN 0-907540-9*
Penguin, 1985. (pbk). ISBN 0-14-008055-4*

Anita Mason
The illusionist
Hamish Hamilton, 1983. ISBN 0-241-10973-6*
Sphere, 1984. (pbk). ISBN 0-349-12279-2*

Salman Rushdie
Shame
Cape, 1983. ISBN 0-224-02952-5*
Pan, 1984. (pbk). ISBN 0-330-28284-0*

Graham Swift
Waterland
Heinemann, 1983. ISBN 0-434-75330-0*
Chivers Press, 1984. (large print ed.).
ISBN 0-86220-114-4*
Pan, 1984. (pbk). ISBN 0-330-28395-2*

Booker Prize

1984

          Anita Brookner
Hotel du lac
Cape, 1984. ISBN 0-224-02238-5*
Granada, 1985. (pbk). ISBN 0-586-06466-4*

shortlist   **J. G. Ballard**
Empire of the sun
Gollancz, 1984. ISBN 0-575-03483-1*
Ulverscroft Large Print Books, 1985.
ISBN 0-7089-8270-0*
Granada, 1985. (pbk). ISBN 0-586-06430-3*

Julian Barnes
Flaubert's parrot
Cape, 1984. ISBN 0-224-02222-9*
Pan, 1985. (pbk). ISBN 0-330-28976-4*

Anita Desai
In custody
Heinemann, 1984. ISBN 0-434-18635-X*
Penguin, 1985. (pbk). ISBN 0-14-007752-9*

Penelope Lively
According to Mark
Heinemann, 1984. ISBN 0-434-42742-X*

David Lodge
Small world
Secker & Warburg, 1984. ISBN 0-436-25663-0*
Penguin, 1985. (pbk). ISBN 0-14-007265-9*

1985

          Keri Hulme
The Bone People
Hodder & Stoughton, 1985.
ISBN 0-340-37024-6*
Pan, 1986. (pbk). ISBN 0-330-29387-7*

shortlist   **Peter Carey**
Illywhacker
Faber & Faber, 1985. ISBN 0-571-13207-3*
Faber & Faber, 1986. (pbk).
ISBN 0-571-13949-3*

J. L. Carr
The Battle of Pollocks Crossing
Viking, 1985. ISBN 0-670-80559-9*
Penguin, 1986. (pbk). ISBN 0-14-007798-7*

Doris Lessing
The good terrorist
Cape, 1985. ISBN 0-224-02323-3*
Grafton, 1986. (pbk). ISBN 0-586-06880-5*

Jan Morris
Last letters from Hav
Viking, 1985. ISBN 0-670-80177-1*
Penguin, 1986. (pbk). ISBN 0-14-006729-9*

Iris Murdoch
The good apprentice
Chatto & Windus, 1985. ISBN 0-7011-3000-8*
Penguin, 1986. (pbk). ISBN 0-14-008699-4*

1986

Kingsley Amis
The old devils
Hutchinson, 1986. ISBN 0-09-163790-2*
Penguin, 1987. (pbk). ISBN 0-14-010133-0*

shortlist

Margaret Atwood
The handmaid's tale
Cape, 1986. ISBN 0-224-02348-9*
G. K. Hall, 1987. (large print ed.).
ISBN 0-8161-4172-X*
Virago, 1987. (pbk). ISBN 0-86068-866-6*

Paul Bailey
Gabriel's lament
Cape, 1986. ISBN 0-224-02823-5*
Penguin, 1987. (pbk). ISBN 0-14-010257-4*

Robertson Davies
What's bred in the bone
Viking, 1986. ISBN 0-670-80916-0*
G. K. Hall, 1987. (large print ed.).
ISBN 0-8161-4133-9*

Kazuo Ishiguro
An artist of the floating world
Faber & Faber, 1986. ISBN 0-571-13608-7*
Faber & Faber, 1987. (pbk).
ISBN 0-571-14716-X*

Timothy Mo
An insular possession
Chatto & Windus, 1986. ISBN 0-7011-3078-4*
Pan, 1987. (pbk). ISBN 0-330-29810-0*

1987

Penelope Lively
Moon tiger
Deutsch, 1987. ISBN 0-233-98107-1*
Penguin, 1988. (pbk). ISBN 0-14-00999-5*

shortlist

Chinua Achebe
Anthills of the Savana
Heinemann, 1987. ISBN 0-434-00604-1*
Pan, 1988. (pbk). ISBN 0-330-30095-4*

Peter Ackroyd
Chatterton
Hamish Hamilton, 1987. ISBN 0-241-12348-8*
Sphere, 1988. (pbk). ISBN 0-349-10008-X*

Nina Bawden
Circles of deceit
Macmillan, 1987. ISBN 0-333-44684-4*
Chivers Press, 1988. (large print ed.).
ISBN 0-7451-7111-7*
Penguin, 1988. (pbk). ISBN 0-14-010741-X*

Brian Moore
The colour of blood
Cape, 1987. ISBN 0-224-02099-4*
Isis Large Print Books, 1988.
ISBN 0-85089-248-2*
Grafton, 1988. (pbk). ISBN 0-586-08739-7*

Iris Murdoch
The book and the brotherhood
Chatto & Windus, 1987. ISBN 0-7011-3251-5
Penguin, 1988. (pbk). ISBN 0-14-010470-4*

1988

          Peter Carey
Oscar and Lucinda
Faber & Faber, 1988. ISBN 0-571-14812-3*
Faber & Faber, 1989. (pbk).
ISBN 0-571-15304-6*

shortlist   **Bruce Chatwin**
Utz
Cape, 1988. ISBN 0-224-02608-9*

Penelope Fitzgerald
The beginning of spring
Collins, 1988. ISBN 0-00-223261-8*
Fontana, 1989. (pbk). ISBN 0-00-654370-7*

David Lodge
Nice work
Secker & Warburg, 1988. ISBN 0-436-25667-3*
Penguin, 1989. (pbk). ISBN 0-14-011920-5*

Salman Rushdie
The Satanic verses
Viking, 1988. ISBN 0-670-82537-9*

Marina Warner
The lost father
Chatto & Windus, 1988. ISBN 0-7011-3220-5*

9 British Film Institute Book Award

The award, of £1,000, which covers the entire range, from academic studies to the more popular titles, was founded to highlight the importance of publishing in achieving a better understanding of the moving image.

Contact British Film Institute
21 St Stephen Street
London W1P 1PL
Tel. 01-255 1444

1984

Phil Hardy
Encyclopaedia of Western movies
Octopus, 1985. ISBN 0-7064-2555-3*

1985

Richard Schickel
D. W. Griffith
Pavilion, 1984. ISBN 0-907516-47-5

1986

Michael Ciment
John Boorman
Faber & Faber, 1986. (pbk). ISBN 0-571-13831-4

1987

Michael Powell
Life in the movies
Heinemann, 1986. ISBN 0-434-59945-X*
Methuen, 1987. (pbk). ISBN 0-413-16510-8*

1988

Leonard J. Leff
Hitchcock and Selznick
Weidenfeld & Nicolson, 1988.
ISBN 0-297-79372-1*
Weidenfeld & Nicolson, 1989. (pbk).
ISBN 0-297-79605-4*

10 The Cheltenham Prize

The prize, of £500, is awarded to the author of any book published in the relevant year, which in the personal opinion of the chosen judge for that year, has received less acclaim than it deserved.

Contact   Cheltenham Festival of Literature
Town Hall
Imperial Square
Cheltenham
Gloucestershire GL50 1QA
Tel. (0242) 521621

1979

Angela Carter
The bloody chamber
Gollancz, 1979. ISBN 0-575-02584-0
Penguin, 1981. (pbk). ISBN 0-14-005404-9*

1980

Thomas Pakenham
The Boer War
Weidenfeld & Nicolson, 1979.
ISBN 0-297-77395-X*
Futura, 1982. (pbk). ISBN 0-7088-1892-7*

1981

D. M. Thomas
The white hotel
Gollancz, 1981. ISBN 0-575-02889-0*
Penguin, 1988. (pbk). ISBN 0-14-010803-3*

1982

Simon Gray
Quartermaine's terms
Methuen, 1981. ISBN 0-413-49140-4
French, 1985. (pbk). ISBN 0-573-11364-5*

1983

Alisdair Gray
Unlikely stories mostly
Canongate, 1983. ISBN 0-86241-029-0
Penguin, 1984. (pbk). ISBN 0-14-006925-9*

Cheltenham Prize

1984

Beatrix Campbell
Wigan Pier revisited
Virago, 1984. (pbk). ISBN 0-86068-417-2*

1985

F. J. M. McLynn
The Jacobite Army in England: 1745, the final campaign
J. Donald, 1983. ISBN 0-85976-093-6*

1986

Frank McGuiness
Observe the sons of Ulster marching towards the Somme
Faber & Faber, 1986. (pbk).
ISBN 0-571-14611-2*

1987

James Kelman
Greyhound for breakfast
Secker & Warburg, 1987. ISBN 0-436-23283-9*
Pan, 1988. (pbk). ISBN 0-330-30027-X*

1988

Peter Robinson
This other life
Carcanet Press, 1988. ISBN 0-85635-737-5*

11 Arthur C. Clarke Award

Made possible by a generous donation from Arthur C. Clarke, the award, of £1,000, is given to the best science fiction novel published in the previous year in either hardback or paperback.

Contact   Science Fiction Foundation
Barking Precinct Library
North East London Polytechnic
Longbridge Road
Dagenham
Essex RM8 2AS
Tel. 01-590 7722 ext. 2177

1986

Margaret Atwood
The handmaid's tale
Cape, 1986. ISBN 0-224-02348-9*
G. K. Hall, 1987. (large print ed.).
ISBN 0-8161-4172-X*
Virago, 1987. (pbk). ISBN 0-86068-866-6*

1987

George Turner
The sea and summer
Faber & Faber, 1987. ISBN 0-571-14846-8*
Faber & Faber, 1989. (pbk).
ISBN 0-586-20358-3*

1988

Rachel Pollock
Unquenchable fire
Century, 1988. ISBN 0-7126-1950-X*
Century, 1989. (pbk). ISBN 0-7126-2341-8*

12 Collins Religious Book Award

Inaugurated in 1969 to commemorate the 150th anniversary of the founding of William Collins & Sons, £2,000 is awarded biennially to the book which, in the opinion of the judges, has made the most distinguished contribution to the relevance of Christianity in the modern world.

Contact William Collins Sons & Co. Ltd
8 Grafton Street
London W1X 3LA
Tel. 01-493 7070

1969

Thomas F. Torrance
Theological science
Oxford University Press, 1969.
ISBN 0-19-213942-8
Oxford University Press, 1978. (pbk).
ISBN 0-19-520083-7*

1971

C. H. Dodd
The founder of Christianity
Collins, 1971. ISBN 0-00-215257-6

1973

John V. Taylor
The go-between God: The Holy Spirit and the Christian mission
SCM Press, 1972. ISBN 0-334-00557-4
SCM Press, 1975. (pbk). ISBN 0-334-00565-5*

1975

Alan Ecclestone
Yes to God
Longman Darton & Tod, 1975.
ISBN 0-232-512991-X*

Collins Religious Book Award

1977
    C. F. D. Moule
The origin of Christianity
Cambridge University Press, 1977.
ISBN 0-521-21290-1*
Cambridge University Press, 1978. (pbk).
ISBN 0-521-29363-4*

1979
    W. H. Vanstone
Love's endeavour, love's expense
Longman Darton & Tod, 1977.
ISBN 0-232-51380-5*

1981
    George B. Caird
The language and imagery of the Bible
Duckworth, 1980. ISBN 0-07156-1444-4*

1983
    Maurice Wiles
Faith and the mystery of God
SCM Press, 1982. (pbk). ISBN 0-334-00477-0*

1985
    Charles Elliot
Praying the kingdom
Longman Darton & Tod, 1985. (pbk).
ISBN 0-232-51645-6*

1987
    Gerald W. Hughes
God of surprises
Longman Darton & Tod, 1985.
ISBN 0-232-51664-2*

13 Commonwealth Writers' Prize

The prize, of £10,000, is for a work of fiction by a citizen of the Commonwealth.

Contact   Book Trust
Book House
45 East Hill
London SW18 2QZ
Tel. 01-870 9055

1987

Olive Senior
Summer lightning and other stories
Longman, 1986. (pbk). ISBN 0-582-78627-4*

runner-up   **Witti Ihimaera**
The matriarch
Heinemann, 1986. ISBN 0-434-36504-1*

1988

Festus Iyayi
Heroes
Longman, 1987. (pbk). ISBN 0-582-78524-3*

runner-up   **George Turner**
The sea and summer
Faber & Faber, 1987. (pbk).
ISBN 0-571-14846-8*
Faber & Faber, 1989. (pbk).
ISBN 0-586-20358-3*

14 Constable Trophy

Supported by the five Northern Regional Arts Associations. The biennial award is for an author of a previously unpublished novel living in the North of England. The winner is presented with the Constable Trophy and £1,000. On acceptance for publication by Constable a further award of £1,000 is given by the publisher as an advance against royalties.

Contact   Northern Arts
10 Osborne Terrace
Jesmond
Newcastle-upon-Tyne NE2 1NZ
Tel. (091) 281 6334

1984

Denise Robertson
Land of lost content: And other stories
Constable, 1985. ISBN 0-09-466440-4
Penguin, 1988. (pbk). ISBN 0-14-010751-7* 1985

Edith French
Connie and Ann
Constable, 1986. ISBN 0-09-467300-4*
Headline Books, 1987. (pbk).
ISBN 0-7472-3046-3*

1986

G. H. Morris
Doves and silk handkerchiefs
Constable, 1987. ISBN 0-09-467940-1*

1988

Paul Sayer
The comforts of madness
Constable, 1988. ISBN 0-09-468480-4*
Hodder & Stoughton, 1989. (pbk).
ISBN 0-340-50804-3*

15 Thomas Cook Travel and Guide Book Awards

The awards, £2,000 for the best travel book and £1,000 for the winning guide book, were founded to encourage the art of travel writing. A new award, of £500, was added in 1988 for the best illustrated travel book.

Contact   Book Trust
                 Book House
                 45 East Hill
                 London SW18 2QZ
                 Tel. 01-870 9055

1980

travel   **Robyn Davidson**
                 Tracks
                 Cape, 1980. ISBN 0-224-01861-2
                 Paladin, 1982. ISBN 0-586-08392-8*

guide   **John Brooks (ed.)**
                 The South American handbook
                 Trade & Travel Publishers. (published annually)

1981

travel   **Jonathan Raban**
                 Old glory
                 Collins, 1981. ISBN 0-00-216521-X*
                 Picador, 1986. (pbk). ISBN 0-00-272778-1*

guide   **Evelyn Garside**
                 China companion
                 Deutsch, 1981. ISBN 0-233-97270-6*

1982

travel   **Tim Severin**
                 The Sinbad voyage
                 Hutchinson, 1982. ISBN 0-09-150560-7
                 Magna Print Books, 1986. (large print ed.).
                 ISBN 0-86009-754-4*

guide		**Geoff Crowther** *India: A travel survival kit* Lonely Planet Publishers, 3rd ed., 1987. ISBN 0-908086-93-8*
1983 travel		**Vikram Seth** *From Heaven lake: Travels through Tibet* Chatto & Windus, 1983. ISBN 0-7011-2700-7 Ulverscroft Large Print Books, 1985. ISBN 0-7089-1290-7*
guide		**Michael Leapman** *Companion guide to New York* Collins, 1983. ISBN 0-00-216198-2 Collins, 1984. (pbk). ISBN 0-00-216394-2*
1984 travel		**Geoffrey Moorhouse** *To the frontier* Hodder & Stoughton, 1984. ISBN 0-340-32349-3* Sceptre, 1988. (pbk). ISBN 0-340-41725-0*
guide		**Hugh McKnight** *Cruising French waterways* Stanford Maritime, 1984. ISBN 0-540-07413-6*
1985 travel		**Patrick Marnham** *So far from God: Journey to Central America* Cape, 1985. ISBN 0-224-02167-2* Isis Large Print Books, 1986. ISBN 1-85089-127-3* Penguin, 1986. (pbk). ISBN 0-14-008556-4*
guide		**Henry Thorold** *Shell guide to Nottinghamshire* Faber & Faber, 1984. ISBN 0-571-13390-8 Faber & Faber, 1984. (pbk). ISBN 0-571-13391-6*

Thomas Cook Travel and Guide Book Awards

1986/7

travel — **Patrick Leigh Fermor**
Between the woods and the water
John Murray, 1986. ISBN 0-7195-4264-2*
Penguin, 1988. (pbk). ISBN 0-14-009430-X*

guide — *Fontana/Hachette guide to France*
Fontana, 1987. (pbk). ISBN 0-00-637156-6*

1988

travel — **Colin Thubron**
Behind the wall: Journey through China
Heinemann, 1987. ISBN 0-434-77988-1*
Penguin, 1988. (pbk). ISBN 0-14-010991-9*

guide — **Stephen Batchelor**
The Tibet guide
Wisdom Publishers, 1987. (pbk).
ISBN 0-86171-046-0*

illustrated — **James Bentley**
Languedoc
George Philip, 1987. ISBN 0-540-01124-X*

1989

travel — **Paul Theroux**
Riding the iron rooster: By train through China
Hamish Hamilton, 1988. ISBN 0-241-12547-2*

guide — **John and Pat Underwood**
Landscapes of Madeira: A countryside guide
3rd ed. Sunflower Books, 1988. (pbk).
ISBN 0-948513-22-5*

illustrated — **Richard B. Fisher**
The Marco Polo expedition: Journey along the Silk Road
Hodder & Stoughton, 1988.
ISBN 0-340-41606-8*

16 Duff Cooper Memorial Prize

£250 awarded annually to a work published in the previous two years of history, biography, politics or poetry which the late Viscount would have enjoyed reading. The prize is a specially bound and inscribed copy of Duff Cooper's autobiography, together with a cheque representing the annual interest on the sum subscribed by his friends to a fund after his death.

Contact The Viscount Norwich
24 Blomfield Road
London W9
Tel. 01-286 5050

1956

Alan Moorehead
Gallipoli
Hamish Hamilton, 1967. BNB B68-02178

1957

Lawrence Durrell
Bitter lemons
Faber & Faber, 1957. BNB B57-4212
Isis Large Print Books, 1986.
ISBN 0-85089-117-6*

1958

John Betjeman
Collected poems
John Murray, 1958. BNB B58-18611
4th ed. John Murray, 1980. (pbk).
ISBN 0-7195-3632-4*

1959

Patrick Leigh Fermor
Mani
John Murray, 1958. ISBN 0-7195-0425-2*
Penguin, 1984. (pbk). ISBN 0-14-009503-9*

Duff Cooper Memorial Prize

1960

Andrew Young
Collected poems
Hart-Davis, 1960. BNB B60-16304

1961

Jocelyn Baines
Joseph Conrad: A critical biography
Greenwood Press, new ed. 1976.
ISBN 0-8371-8304-9*
Penguin, 1986. (pbk). ISBN 0-14-058018-2*

1962

Michael Howard
The Franco-Prussian War: The German invasion of France, 1870–1
Hart-Davies, 1961. BNB B61-16764
Methuen, 1981. (pbk). ISBN 0-416-30750-7*

1963

Aileen Ward
John Keats: The making of a poet
Secker & Warburg, 1963. BNB B63-17513

1964

Ivan Morris
The world of the Shining Prince: Court life in ancient Japan
Oxford University Press, 1964. BNB B64-12118
Penguin, 1969. (pbk). ISBN 0-14-055083-6*

1965

George Painter
Marcel Proust: A biography
Chatto & Windus, 1965. BNB B65-12190

1966

Nirad C. Chaudhuri
The Continent of Circe: Being an essay on the peoples of India
Chatto & Windus, 1965. BNB B65-19854

1967

J. A. Baker
The peregrine
Collins, 1967. BNB B67-05384

1968

Roy Fuller
New poems
Deutsch, 1968. ISBN 0-233-96025-2

1969

John Gross
The rise and fall of the man of letters: Aspects of English literary life since 1800
Weidenfeld & Nicolson, 1969.
ISBN 0-297-76494-2

1970

Enid McLeod
Charles of Orleans: Prince and poet
Chatto & Windus, 1969. ISBN 0-7011-1757-5

1971

Geoffrey Grigson
Discoveries of bones and stones and other poems
Macmillan, 1971. ISBN 0-333-12582-7

1972

Quentin Bell
Virginia Woolf
Vol.1 Hogarth Press, 1972.
ISBN 0-7012-0291-2
Vol.2 Hogarth Press, 1972.
ISBN 0-7012-0371-4
Grafton, 1987. (pbk). ISBN 0-586-08676-5*

1973

Robin Lane-Fox
Alexander the Great
Allen Lane, 1973. ISBN 0-7139-0500-X
Penguin, 1986. (pbk). ISBN 0-14-008878-4*

1974

Jon Stallworthy
Wilfred Owen
Oxford University Press, 1974.
ISBN 0-19-211719-X

Duff Cooper Memorial Prize

1975
Seamus Heaney
North
Faber & Faber, 1975. ISBN 0-571-10564-5
Faber & Faber, 1975. (pbk).
ISBN 0-571-10813-X*

1976
Denis Mack Smith
Mussolini's Roman Empire
Longman, 1976. ISBN 0-582-50266-7

1977
Eric Robertson Dodds
Missing persons: An autobiography
Oxford University Press, 1977.
ISBN 0-19-812086-9*

1978
Mark Girouard
Life in the English country house: A social and architectural history
Yale University Press, 1978.
ISBN 0-300-02273-5*
Penguin, 1980. (pbk). ISBN 0-14-005406-5*

1979
Geoffrey Hill
Tenebrae
Deutsch, 1978. ISBN 0-233-97049-5*

1980
Robert Bernard Martin
Tennyson: The unquiet heart
Oxford University Press, 1980.
ISBN 0-19-812072-9*
Faber & Faber, 1983. (pbk).
ISBN 0-571-11842-9*

1981
Victoria Glendinning
Edith Sitwell: A unicorn among the lions
Weidenfeld & Nicolson, 1981.
ISBN 0-297-77801-3
Oxford University Press, 1983. (pbk).
ISBN 0-19-281369-2*

Duff Cooper Memorial Prize

1982

Richard Ellmann
James Joyce
2nd ed. Oxford University Press, 1982.
ISBN 0-19-503103-2*
2nd ed. Oxford University Press, 1984. (pbk).
ISBN 0-19-211965-6*

1983

Peter Porter
Collected poems
Oxford University Press, 1983.
ISBN 0-19-211948-6*
Oxford University Press, 1984. (pbk).
ISBN 0-19-211965-6*

1984

Hilary Spurling
Secrets of a woman's heart: The later life of Ivy Compton-Burnett, 1920–1969
Hodder & Stoughton, 1984.
ISBN 0-340-26241-9*
Penguin, 1985. (pbk). ISBN 0-14-058013-1*

1985

Ann Thwaite
Edmund Gosse: A literary landscape, 1849–1928
Secker & Warburg, 1984. ISBN 0-436-52146-6
Oxford University Press, 1985. (pbk).
ISBN 0-19-281898-8*

1986

Alan Crawford
C. R. Ashbee: Architect, designer and romantic socialist
Yale University Press, 1985.
ISBN 0-300-03467-9*

1987

Robert Hughes
The fatal shore: History of the transportation of convicts to Australia, 1787–1868
Collins Harvill, 1987. ISBN 0-00-217361-1*
Pan, 1988. (pbk). ISBN 0-330-29892-5*

Duff Cooper Memorial Prize

1988

Humphrey Carpenter
Serious character: Life of Ezra Pound
Faber & Faber, 1988. ISBN 0-571-14786-0*

17 The Crime Writers' Association Awards

The Association has been presenting awards since 1955. The winning titles are chosen from shortlists submitted by the members of an independent panel chosen by the Committee each year. From 1969 onwards the Gold Dagger: £1,000 and a gold plated dagger, has been presented for the best crime book of the year with the Silver Dagger: £500 and a silver plated dagger, going to the runner-up. Since 1973 the John Creasey Memorial Award has been presented to the best first novel and from 1978 a Gold Dagger has been awarded to the best non-fiction crime book. The latest award has been sponsored by the *Police review* for authenticity in crime fiction dealing with police procedure.

Contact Crime Writers' Association
PO Box 172
Tring
Hertfordshire HP23 5LP

1955

Winston Graham
The little walls
Bodley Head, new ed. 1972.
ISBN 0-370-01464-2*
Fontana, 1969. (pbk). ISBN 0-00-611964-6*

1956

Edward Grierson
The second man
Chatto & Windus, 1956. BNB B56-04083

1957

Julian Symons
The colour of murder
Collins, 1957. BNB B57-08237
Ulverscroft Large Print Books, 1988.
ISBN 0-7089-1750-X*
Papermac, 1988. (pbk). ISBN 0-333-46635-7*

1958

Margot Bennett
Someone from the past
Eyre & Spottiswoode, 1958. BNB B58-07623

65

1959

    Eric Ambler
    Passage of arms
    Heinemann, 1959. ISBN 0-434-01973-9
    Fontana, 1989. (pbk). ISBN 0-00-617072-2*

1960

    Lionel Davidson
    The night of Wenceslas
    Gollancz, 1960. BNB B60-00637

1961

    Mary Kelly
    The spoilt kill
    Michael Joseph, 1961. BNB B61-09550

1962

    Joan Fleming
    When I grow rich
    Collins, 1962. ISBN 0-00-231994-2*

1963

    John le Carré
    The spy who came in from the cold
    Gollancz, 1963. ISBN 0-575-02900-5
    Hutchinson Educational, 1966.
    ISBN 0-09-076870-1*
    Hutchinson Education, 1974. (pbk).
    ISBN 0-09-120131-4*
    Pan, 1965. (pbk). ISBN 0-330-20107-7*

1964–1969 awards were given alternately for the best British and the best foreign novel.

1964

    H. R. F. Keating
    The perfect murder
    Collins, new ed. 1981.
    ISBN 0-00-231683-8*
    Mysterious Press, 1987. (pbk).
    ISBN 0-09-952800-2*

Crime Writers' Association Awards

best foreign		**Patricia Highsmith** *The two faces of January* Heinemann, 1964. ISBN 0-434-33506-1* Penguin, 1988. (pbk). ISBN 0-14-010117-9*

1965

Ross Macdonald
The far side of the dollar
Collins, 1965. BNB B65-16728
John Curley, 1980. (large print ed.).
ISBN 0-89340-248-6*
Allison & Busby, 1988. (pbk).
ISBN 0-85031-714-2*

best British   **Gavin Lyall**
Midnight plus one
Hodder & Stoughton, 1965. BNB B65-05149
Pan, 1967. (pbk). ISBN 0-330-10530-2*

1966

Lionel Davidson
A long way to Shiloh
Gollancz, 1966. BNB B66-13563

best foreign   **John Ball**
In the heat of the night
Michael Joseph, 1966. BNB B66-00899

1967

Emma Lathen
Murder against the grain
Gollancz, 1967. BNB B67-23142

best British   **Eric Ambler**
Dirty story
Bodley Head, 1967. BNB B67-19691
Fontana, 1969. (pbk). ISBN 0-00-611998-0*

1968

Peter Dickinson
Skin deep
Hodder & Stoughton, 1968.
ISBN 0-340-02995-1

Crime Writers' Association Awards

best foreign
Sebastian Japrisot
The lady in the car with glasses and a gun
Souvenir Press, 1968. ISBN 0-285-50076-7*

1969
gold dagger
Peter Dickinson
A pride of heroes
Hodder & Stoughton, 1969. ISBN 0-340-04260-5
Mysterious Press, 1988. (pbk).
ISBN 0-09-941620-4*

silver dagger
Francis Clifford
Another way of dying
Hodder & Stoughton, 1968. ISBN 0-340-04257-5

best foreign
Rex Stout
The father hunt
Collins, 1969. ISBN 0-00-231234-6
G. K. Hall, 1983. (large print ed.).
ISBN 0-8161-3548-7*

1970
gold dagger
Joan Fleming
Young man, I think you're dying
Collins, 1970. ISBN 0-00-231950-0
John Curley, 1980. (large print ed.).
ISBN 0-89340-058-0*

silver dagger
Anthony Price
The labyrinth makers
Gollancz, new ed. 1983. ISBN 0-575-03388-6*
Ulverscroft Large Print Books, 1981.
ISBN 0-7089-0711-2*

1971
gold dagger
James McClure
The steam pig
Gollancz, 1971. ISBN 0-575-00770-2
Hodder & Stoughton, 1989. (pbk).
ISBN 0-340-48904-9*

Crime Writers' Association Awards

silver dagger		**P. D. James** *Shroud for a nightingale* Faber & Faber, 1971. ISBN 0-571-09719-7 G. K. Hall, 1982. (large print ed.). ISBN 0-8161-6791-5*
1972 gold dagger		**Eric Ambler** *The Levanter* Weidenfeld & Nicolson, 1972. ISBN 0-297-99521-9* Fontana, 1988. (pbk). ISBN 0-00-617069-2*
silver dagger		**Victor Canning** *The rainbird pattern* Heinemann, 1972. ISBN 0-434-10773-5*
1973 gold dagger		**Robert Littell** *The defection of A. J. Lewinter* Hodder & Stoughton, 1973. ISBN 0-340-17636-9
silver dagger		**Gwendoline Butler** *A coffin for Pandora* Macmillan, 1973. ISBN 0-333-14889-4
John Creasey award		**Kyril Bonfiglioli** *Don't point that thing at me* Weidenfeld & Nicolson, 1972. ISBN 0-297-99520-0
1974 gold dagger		**Anthony Price** *Other paths of glory* Gollancz, 1974. ISBN 0-575-01878-X Futura, 1982. (pbk). ISBN 0-7088-2187-1*
silver dagger		**Francis Clifford** *The Grosvenor Square goodbye* Hodder & Stoughton, 1974. ISBN 0-340-18536-8

Crime Writers' Association Awards

John Creasey award	**Roger L. Simon** *The big fix* Deutsch, 1974. ISBN 0-233-96587-4*
1975 gold dagger	**Nicholas Meyer** *The seven per cent solution* Hodder & Stoughton, 1975. ISBN 0-340-19414-6 Ulverscroft Large Print Books, 1977. ISBN 0-7089-0052-6*
silver dagger	**P. D. James** *The black tower* Faber & Faber, 1975. ISBN 0-571-10731-1 G. K. Hall, 1982. (large print ed.). ISBN 0-8161-6789-3*
John Creasey award	**Sara George** *Acid drop* Macmillan, 1975. ISBN 0-333-18054-2
1976 gold dagger	**Ruth Rendell** *A demon in my view* Hutchinson, 1976. ISBN 0-09-126100-7* Arrow, 1977. (pbk). ISBN 0-09-914860-9*
silver dagger	**James McClure** *Rogue eagle* Macmillan, 1976. ISBN 0-333-19698-8
John Creasey award	**Patrick Alexander** *Death of a thin-skinned animal* Macmillan, 1976. ISBN 0-333-21249-5
1977 gold dagger	**John le Carré** *The honourable schoolboy* Hodder & Stoughton, 1977. ISBN 0-340-22042-2* Chivers Press, 1987. (large print ed.). ISBN 0-86220-222-1* G. K. Hall, 1978. (large print ed.). ISBN 0-8161-6539-4* Pan, 1979. (pbk). ISBN 0-330-25356-5*

Crime Writers' Association Awards

1977
silver dagger   **William McIlvanney**
Laidlaw
Magna Print Books, 1986. (large print ed.).
ISBN 0-86009-999-7*
Hodder & Stoughton, 1979. (pbk).
ISBN 0-340-23670-1*

John Creasey   **Jonathan Cash**
Award   *The Judas pair*
Ulverscroft Large Print Books, 1982.
ISBN 0-7089-0856-X*
Arrow, 1986. (pbk). ISBN 0-09-947070-5*

1978
gold dagger   **Lionel Davidson**
The Chelsea murders
Cape, 1978. ISBN 0-224-01532-X

silver dagger   **Peter Lovesey**
Waxwork
Macmillan, 1978. ISBN 0-333-23455-3
Ulverscroft Large Print Books, 1980.
ISBN 0-7089-0394-0*
Mysterious Press, 1988. (pbk).
ISBN 0-09-956060-7*

John Creasey   **Paula Gosling**
Award   *A running duck*
Macmillan, 1978. ISBN 0-333-23721-8*
Ulverscroft Large Print Books, 1981.
ISBN 0-7089-0618-4*

1979
gold dagger   **Dick Francis**
Whip hand
Michael Joseph, 1979. ISBN 0-7181-1845-6
Pan, 1981. (pbk). ISBN 0-330-26306-4*

silver dagger   **Colin Dexter**
Service of all the dead
Macmillan, 1979. ISBN 0-333-27002-9*
Pan, 1980. (pbk). ISBN 0-330-26148-7*

Crime Writers' Association Awards

John Creasey Award
: **David Serafin**
Saturday of glory
Collins, 1979. ISBN 0-00-231793-1
Ulverscroft Large Print Books, 1981.
ISBN 0-7089-0577-3*

1980

gold dagger
: **H. R. F. Keating**
The murder of the Maharajah
G. K. Hall, 1981. (large print ed.).
ISBN 0-8161-3179-1*
Mysterious Press, 1988. (pbk).
ISBN 0-09-952810-X*

silver dagger
: **Ellis Peters**
Monk's hood
Macmillan, 1980. ISBN 0-333-29410-6*
Ulverscroft Large Print Books, 1982.
ISBN 0-7089-0829-2*
Futura, 1984. (pbk). ISBN 0-7088-2553-2*

John Creasey Award
: **Liza Cody**
Dupe
Collins, 1980. ISBN 0-00-231272-7*

1981

gold dagger
: **Martin Cruz Smith**
Gorky Park
Collins, 1981. ISBN 0-00-222278-7*
G. K. Hall, 1982. (large print ed.).
ISBN 0-8161-3295-X*
Pan, 1982. (pbk). ISBN 0-330-26673-X*

silver dagger
: **Colin Dexter**
The dead of Jericho
Macmillan, 1981. ISBN 0-333-31728-9*
Pan, 1983. (pbk). ISBN 0-330-26693-4*

John Creasey Award
: **James Leigh**
The Ludi victor
Bodley Head, 1981. ISBN 0-370-30373-3
Triad, 1982. (pbk). ISBN 0-586-05397-2*

Crime Writers' Association Awards

gold dagger
non-fiction
Jacob Timerman
Prisoner without a name, cell without a number
Weidenfeld & Nicolson, 1981.
ISBN 0-297-77995-8

1982
gold dagger
Peter Lovesey
The false Inspector Drew
Macmillan, 1982. ISBN 0-333-32748-9*
Chivers Press, 1988. (large print ed.).
ISBN 0-86220-269-8*
Arrow, 1983. (pbk). ISBN 0-09-931560-2

silver dagger
S. T. Hayman
Ritual murder
Constable, 1982. ISBN 0-09-465880-3

John Creasey
Award
Andrew Taylor
Caroline miniscule
Gollancz, 1972. ISBN 0-575-03142-5*

gold dagger
non-fiction
John Cornwell
Earth to earth: The true story of the lives and violent deaths of a Devon farming family
Allen Lane, 1982. ISBN 0-7139-1045-3
Ulverscroft Large Print Books, 1987.
ISBN 0-7089-1609-0*

1983
gold dagger
John Hutton
Accidental crimes
Bodley Head, 1983. ISBN 0-370-30498-5
Chivers Press, 1986. (large print ed.).
ISBN 0-85119-380-3*

silver dagger
William McIlvanney
The papers of Tony Veitch
Hodder & Stoughton, 1983.
ISBN 0-340-22907-1*
Magna Print Books, 1987. (large print ed.).
ISBN 1-85057-035-3*
Hodder & Stoughton, 1984. (pbk).
ISBN 0-340-35472-0*

Crime Writers' Association Awards

John Creasey Award	**Carol Clemeau** *The Adriatic Club: A classical mystery* Collins, 1982. ISBN 0-00-231034-1
gold dagger non-fiction	**Peter Watson** *Double dealer* Hutchinson, 1983. ISBN 0-09-147080-3

1984

gold dagger	**B. M. Gill** *The twelfth juror* Hodder & Stoughton, 1984. ISBN 0-340-34938-7* Hodder & Stoughton, 1985. (pbk). ISBN 0-340-38520-0*
silver dagger	**Ruth Rendell** *The tree of hands* Hutchinson, 1984. ISBN 0-09-158680-1* Chivers Press, 1986. (large print ed.). ISBN 0-85119-370-6* Arrow, 1985. (pbk). ISBN 0-09-943470-9*
John Creasey Award	**Elizabeth Ironside** *A very private enterprise* Hodder & Stoughton, 1984. ISBN 0-340-35269-8 Fontana, 1986. (pbk). ISBN 0-00-617280-6*
gold dagger non-fiction	**David Yallop** *In God's name* Cape, 1984. ISBN 0-224-02089-7* Corgi, 1987. (pbk). ISBN 0-552-13288-8*

1985

gold dagger	**Paula Gosling** *Monkey puzzle* Macmillan, 1985. ISBN 0-333-38659-0* Ulverscroft Large Print Books, 1986. ISBN 0-7089-1487-X* Pan, 1985. (pbk). ISBN 0-330-28943-8*

Crime Writers' Association Awards

silver dagger	**Dorothy Simpson** *Last seen alive* Michael Joseph, 1985. ISBN 0-7181-2520-7 Ulverscroft Large Print Books, 1986. ISBN 0-7089-1508-6*
John Creasey Award	**Robert Richardson** *The Latimer mercy* Gollancz, 1985. ISBN 0-575-03703-2
gold dagger non-fiction	**Brian Masters** *Killing for company* Cape, 1985. ISBN 0-224-02184-2* Hodder & Stoughton, 1986. (pbk). ISBN 0-340-38634-7*

1986

gold dagger	**Ruth Rendell** *Live flesh* Hutchinson, 1980. ISBN 0-09-163680-9* Arrow, 1987. (pbk). ISBN 0-09-925530-8*
silver dagger	**P. D. James** *A taste for death* Faber & Faber, 1986. ISBN 0-571-13799-7* Chivers Press, 1987. (large print ed.). ISBN 0-86220-205-1*
John Creasey Award	**Neville Steed** *Tinplate* Weidenfeld & Nicolson, 1986. ISBN 0-297-78802-7* Chivers Press, 1988. (large print ed.). ISBN 0-7451-9377-3* Mysterious Press, 1988. ISBN 0-09-957750-X*
gold dagger non-fiction	**John Bryson** *Evil angels* Viking, 1986. ISBN 0-670-80993-4*
Police Review Award	**Bill Knox** *The crossfire killings* Century, 1986. ISBN 0-7126-9454-4* Ulverscroft Large Print Books, 1987. ISBN 0-7089-1849-2*

Crime Writers' Association Awards

1987

gold dagger
Barbara Vine
A fatal inversion
Viking, 1987. ISBN 0-670-80977-2*
Penguin, 1988. (pbk). ISBN 0-14-008637-4*

silver dagger
Scott Turow
Presumed innocent
Bloomsbury Press, 1987. ISBN 0-7475-0033-9*
Chivers Press, 1988. (large print ed.).
ISBN 0-7451-7137-0*
Penguin, 1988. (pbk). ISBN 0-14-010336-8*

John Creasey Award
Denis Kilcommons
Dark apostle
Bantam, 1987. ISBN 0-593-01307-7*
Magna Print Books, 1988. (large print ed.).
ISBN 1-85057-446-1*
Magna Print Books, 1988. (large print ed.).
ISBN 1-85057-447-2*
Corgi, 1988. (pbk). ISBN 0-552-13211-X*

gold dagger non-fiction
Bernard Taylor
Perfect murder: A century of unsolved homicides
Grafton, 1987. ISBN 0-246-13192-6*
Grafton, 1988. (pbk). ISBN 0-586-05587-8*

1988

gold dagger
Michael Dibdin
Ratking
Faber & Faber, 1988. ISBN 0-571-15147-7*
Faber & Faber, 1989. (pbk).
ISBN 0-571-15421-2*

silver dagger
Sara Paretsky
Toxic shock
Gollancz, 1988. ISBN 0-575-04372-5*

John Creasey Award
Janet Neel
Death's bright angel
Constable, 1988. ISBN 0-09-468160-0*

Crime Writers' Association Awards

gold dagger **Bernard Wasserstein**
non-fiction *Secret lives of Trebitsch Lincoln*
Yale University Press, 1988.
ISBN 0-300-04076-8*

18 Hunter Davies Prize for the Lakeland Book of the Year

Created by the Cumbria Tourist Board and Hunter Davies in 1984, the prize of £100 is given to the best book on Cumbria and the Lake District.

Contact   Cumbria Tourist Board
Ashleigh
Holly Road
Windermere
Cumbria LA23 2AQ
Tel. (09662) 4444

1984

Automobile Association/Ordnance Survey
Guide to the Lake District
Automobile Association, 1984.
ISBN 0-86145-226-7*
Automobile Association, 1984. (pbk).
ISBN 0-86145-192-9*

1985

Alfred Wainwright
Fellwalking with Wainwright: Eighteen of the author's favourite walks in Lakeland
Michael Joseph, 1984. ISBN 0-7181-2428-6*
Michael Joseph, 1988. (pbk).
ISBN 0-7181-2771-4*

Christina Hardyment
Arthur Ransome and Captain Flint's trunk
Cape, 1984. ISBN 0-224-02989-4*
Cape, 1988. (pbk). ISBN 0-224-02590-2*

1986/7

Peter Thornton
Lakeland from the air
Dalesman, 1986. ISBN 0-85206-850-6*
Dalesman, 1986. (pbk). ISBN 0-85206-901-4*

Trevor Haywood
Walking with a camera in Herries' Lakeland
Fountain Press, 1986. ISBN 0-86343-023-6*

1988

        Molly Lefebure
The bondage of love: A biography of Mrs Samuel Taylor Coleridge
Gollancz, 1986. ISBN 0-575-03871-3*
Gollancz, 1988. (pbk). ISBN 0-575-04223-0*

19 Mary Elgin Award

Mary Elgin was an author of traditional romantic suspense stories for women. On her death her husband inaugurated in her memory an annual prize of £50 for new novelists writing in a similar vein. Though it does not have to be a first novel the emphasis is on encouraging new writers. The award is not advertised externally and is awarded to a new author usually on the Hodder & Stoughton fiction list from a shortlist judged by Mary Elgin's husband.

Contact   Hodder & Stoughton
            47 Bedford Square
            London WC1B 3DP
            Tel. 01-636 9851

1970

            Gillian Tindall
            Someone else
            Hodder & Stoughton, 1969. ISBN 0-340-10710-3

1971

            Jay Gilbert
            An edge to the laughter
            Hodder & Stoughton, 1971. ISBN 0-340-12575-6

1972   No Award

1973

            Phyllis Gant
            Islands
            Hodder & Stoughton, 1973. ISBN 0-340-16536-7

1974

            Frances Murray
            The burning lamp
            Hodder & Stoughton, 1973. ISBN 0-340-17953-8

1975

            Anne Worboys
            The lion of Delos
            Hodder & Stoughton, 1975. ISBN 0-340-19132-5
            Ulverscroft Large Print Books, 1980.
            ISBN 0-7089-0500-5*

Mary Elgin Award

1976
    Sarah Neilan
    The Braganza pursuit
    Hodder & Stoughton, 1976. ISBN 0-340-20581-4
    Ulverscroft Large Print Books, 1984.
    ISBN 0-7089-1076-9*

1977
    Roseleen Milne
    Borrowed plumes
    Hodder & Stoughton, 1977. ISBN 0-340-21741-3

1978
    Katherine Gordon
    The emerald peacock
    Ulverscroft Large Print Books, 1979.
    ISBN 0-7089-0329-0*
    Hodder & Stoughton, 1980. (pbk).
    ISBN 0-340-25376-2*

1979   No Award

1980
    Margaret Evans
    And the little hills rejoice
    Hodder & Stoughton, 1979. ISBN 0-340-22894-6
    Magna Print Books, 1984. (large print ed.).
    ISBN 0-86009-561-4*

1981
    Catherine Dunbar
    The nuthatch tree
    Hodder & Stoughton, 1981.
    ISBN 0-340-26246-X*

1982   No Award

1983
    Dawn Lowe-Watson
    The sound of water
    Hodder & Stoughton, 1982. ISBN 0-340-28166-9

Mary Elgin Award

1984

    Barbara Whitnell
    The song of the rainbird
    Hodder & Stoughton, 1984. ISBN 0-340-33241-7

1985

    Elizabeth Ironside
    A very private enterprise
    Hodder & Stoughton, 1984.
    ISBN 0-340-35269-8*
    Fontana, 1986. (pbk). ISBN 0-00-617280-6*

1986 – 87   No Award

1988

    Rosumunde Pilcher
    The shell seekers
    Severn House, 1985. ISBN 0-7278-1148-7
    Chivers Press, 1985. (large print ed.).
    ISBN 0-7451-0156-9*
    Hodder & Stoughton, 1989 (pbk).
    ISBN 0-340-49181-7*
    Sphere, 1986. (pbk). ISBN 0-7221-6867-5*

20 Geoffrey Faber Memorial Prize

£500 awarded in alternate years to works of prose fiction and poetry first published in the UK during the previous two years. Authors, resident in the UK, British Commonwealth, the Republic of Ireland and South Africa, must be under 40 at the time of publication.

Contact Faber & Faber
3 Queen Square
London WC1N 3AU
Tel. 01-278 6881

1964
poetry

Christopher Middleton
Torse 3: Poems 1949-1961
Longman, 1962. BNB B62-04354

George Macbeth
The broken places: poems
Scorpion Press, 1963. BNB B63-07268

1965
fiction

Frank Tuohy
The ice saints
Macmillan, 1964. BNB B64-11998

1966
poetry

Jon Silkin
Nature with man
Chatto & Windus, 1965. BNB B65-10807

1967
fiction

William McIlvanney
Remedy is none
Eyre & Spottiswoode, 1966. BNB B66-10590

John Noone
The man with the chocolate egg
Hamish Hamilton, 1966. BNB B66-07525
Penguin, 1973. (pbk). ISBN 0-14-003287-8*

Geoffrey Faber Memorial Prize

1968
poetry

Seamus Heaney
Death of a naturalist
Faber & Faber, 1966. BNB B66-09171
Faber & Faber, 1969. (pbk). ISBN 0-571-09024-9*

1969
fiction

Piers Paul Read
The junkers
Secker & Warburg, 1968. ISBN 0-436-40970-4*

1970
poetry

Geoffrey Hill
King Log
Deutsch, 1968. ISBN 0-233-96021-X

1971
fiction

J. G. Farrell
Troubles
Cape, 1970. ISBN 0-224-61900-4
Fontana, 1984. (pbk). ISBN 0-00-654046-5*

1972
poetry

Tony Harrison
The loiners
London Magazine Editions, 1970.
ISBN 0-900626-19-4

1973
fiction

David Storey
Pasmore
Cape, 1986. ISBN 0-224-02840-5*

1974
poetry

John Fuller
Cannibals and missionaries
Secker & Warburg, 1972. ISBN 0-436-16802-2

Epistles to several persons
Secker & Warburg, 1973. ISBN 0-436-16804-9

Geoffrey Faber Memorial Prize

1975
fiction

Richard Wright
In the middle of a life
Macmillan, 1973. ISBN 0-333-15599-8

1976
poetry

Douglas Dunn
Love or nothing
Faber & Faber, 1974. ISBN 0-571-10614-5

1977
fiction

Carolyn Slaughter
The story of the weasel
Hart-Davis MacGibbon, 1976.
ISBN 0-246-10887-8

1978
poetry

David Harsent
Dreams of the dead
Oxford University Press, 1977. (pbk).
ISBN 0-19-211875-7

Kit Wright
The bear looked over the mountain
Salamander, 1977. ISBN 0-904632-11-3

1979
fiction

Timothy Mo
The monkey king
Deutsch, 1978. ISBN 0-233-97007-X
Abacus, 1984. (pbk). ISBN 0-349-12393-4*

1980
poetry

George Szirtes
The slant door
Secker & Warburg, 1979. ISBN 0-436-50997-0

Hugo Williams
Love lift
Deutsch, 1979. ISBN 0-233-97175-0

Geoffrey Faber Memorial Prize

1981
fiction

J. M. Coetzee
Waiting for the barbarians
Secker & Warburg, 1980. ISBN 0-436-10295-1*
Penguin, 1982. (pbk). ISBN 0-14-006555-5*

1982
poetry

Paul Muldoon
Why Brownlee left
Faber & Faber, 1980. (pbk). ISBN 0-571-11592-6*

Tom Paulin
The strange museum
Faber & Faber, 1980. (pbk). ISBN 0-571-11511-X*

1983
fiction

Graham Swift
Shuttlecock
Allen Lane, 1981. ISBN 0-7139-1413-0
Penguin, 1982. (pbk). ISBN 0-14-006322-6*

1984
poetry

James Fenton
In memory of war: Poems 1968-83
Salamander, 1984. ISBN 0-907540-17-1
Penguin, 1983. (pbk). ISBN 0-14-006812-0*

1985
fiction

Julian Barnes
Flaubert's parrot
Cape, 1984. ISBN 0-224-02222-9*
Pan, 1985. (pbk). ISBN 0-330-28976-4*

1986
poetry

David Scott
A quiet gathering
Bloodaxe, 1984. ISBN 0-906427-68-1*

1987
fiction

Guy Vanderhaeghe
Man descending
Bodley Head, 1986. ISBN 0-370-30718-6*

Geoffrey Faber Memorial Prize

1988
poetry   **Michael Hofman**
Acrimony: Poems
Faber & Faber, 1986. ISBN 0-571-14527-2*
Faber & Faber, 1986. (pbk).
ISBN 0-571-14528-0*

1989
fiction   **David Profumo**
Sea music
Secker & Warburg, 1988. ISBN 0-436-38714-X*
Sceptre, 1989. (pbk). ISBN 0-340-49937-0*

21 The Fawcett Society Book Prize

The prize, of £500, is awarded to works of fiction and non-fiction alternately, which illuminate women's position in society today and contribute to an understanding of recent changes in roles, pursuits, interests or attitudes.

Contact	The General Secretary The Fawcett Society 46 Harleyford Road London SE11 5AY Tel. 01-587 1287

1982
non-fiction

Margaret Stacey and Marion Price
Women, power and politics
Tavistock, 1981. ISBN 0-422-76140-0*
Tavistock, 1981. (pbk). ISBN 0-422-76150-8*

1983
fiction

Pat Barker
Union Street
Virago, 1982. ISBN 0-86068-282-X
Virago, 1982. (pbk). ISBN 0-86068-283-8*

1984
non-fiction

Carolyn Steedman
Tidy house: Little girls writing
Virago, 1983. ISBN 0-86068-321-4*
Virago, 1983. (pbk). ISBN 0-86068-326-5*

1985
fiction

Zoe Fairbairns
Here today
Methuen, 1984. ISBN 0-413-53080-9
Methuen, 1985. (pbk). ISBN 0-413-57930-1*

Fawcett Society Book Prize

1986
non-fiction
Marina Warner
Monuments and maidens: The allegory of the female form
Weidenfeld & Nicolson, 1985.
ISBN 0-297-78408-0*
Pan, 1987. (pbk). ISBN 0-330-29675-2*

1987
fiction
Shena Mackay
Redhill rococo
Heinemann, 1987. ISBN 0-434-44046-9
Sphere, 1987. (pbk). ISBN 0-349-12271-7*

1988
non-fiction
Beatrix Campbell
Iron ladies: Why women vote Tory
Virago, 1987. (pbk). ISBN 0-86068-689-2*

22 *Guardian* Fiction Prize

£1,000 awarded for a novel by a British or Commonwealth writer.

Contact Literary Editor
The Guardian
119 – 141 Farringdon Road
London EC1R 3ER
Tel. 01-278 2332

1965

Clive Barry
Crumb borne
Faber & Faber, 1965. BNB B65-08641

1966

Archie Hind
The dear green place
New Authors, 1966. BNB B66-03373
Polygon Books, 1984. (pbk).
ISBN 0-904919-81-1*

1967

Eva Figes
Winter journey
Faber & Faber, 1967. BNB B67-07088

1968

P. J. Kavanagh
A song and dance
Chatto & Windus, 1968. ISBN 0-7011-1401-0*

1969

Maurice Leitch
Poor Lazarus
MacGibbon & Kee, 1969. ISBN 0-261-61830-X

1970

Margaret Blount
When did you last see your father?
Hutchinson, 1970. ISBN 0-09-101920-6

Guardian Fiction Prize

1971

Thomas Kilroy
The big chapel
Faber & Faber, 1971. ISBN 0-571-09700-6

1972

John Berger
G
Weidenfeld & Nicolson, 1972.
ISBN 0-297-99423-9
Hogarth Press, 1989. (pbk). ISBN 0-7012-0833-3*

1973

Peter Redgrove
In the country of the skin
Routledge & Kegan Paul, 1973.
ISBN 0-7100-5714-6*

1974

Beryl Bainbridge
The bottle factory outing
Duckworth, 1974. ISBN 0-7156-0864-9*
Fontana, 1985. (pbk). ISBN 0-00-654100-3*

1975

Sylvia Clayton
Friends and Romans
Faber & Faber, 1975. ISBN 0-571-10728-1

1976

Robert Nye
Falstaff: Being the 'acta domini Johannis John Fastolfe', or, 'Life and valiant deeds of Sir John Faustoff', or, 'The Hundred Days War'
Hamish Hamilton, 1976. ISBN 0-241-89429-8

1977

Michael Moorcock
The condition of muzak: A Jerry Cornelius novel
Allison & Busby, 1977. ISBN 0-85031-044-X

Guardian Fiction Prize

1978

Roy A. K. Heath
The murderer
Allison & Busby, 1978. ISBN 0-85031-228-0
Fontana, 1984. (pbk). ISBN 0-00-654077-5*

1979

Neil Jordan
Night in Tunisia: And other stories
Writers & Readers, 1979. ISBN 0-904613-56-9

1980

J. L. Carr
A month in the country
Harvester Press, 1980. ISBN 0-85527-328-3*
Isis Large Print Books, 1988.
ISBN 0-85089-253-9*

1981

John Banville
Kepler
Secker & Warburg, 1981. ISBN 0-436-03264-3*
Granada, 1983. (pbk). ISBN 0-586-05778-1*

1982

Glyn Hughes
Where I used to play on the green
Gollancz, 1982. ISBN 0-575-02997-8

1983

Graham Swift
Waterland
Heinemann, 1983. ISBN 0-434-75330-0*
Chivers Press, 1984. (large print ed.).
ISBN 0-86220-114-4*
Pan, 1984. (pbk). ISBN 0-330-28395-2*

1984

J. G. Ballard
The empire of the sun
Gollancz, 1984. ISBN 0-575-03483-1*
Ulverscroft Large Print Books, 1985.
ISBN 0-7089-8270-0*
Granada, 1985. (pbk). ISBN 0-586-06430-3*

Guardian Fiction Prize

1985

    Peter Ackroyd
    Hawksmoor
    Hamish Hamilton, 1985. ISBN 0-241-11664-3*
    Sphere, 1986. (pbk). ISBN 0-349-10057-8*

1986

    Jim Crace
    Continent
    Heinemann, 1986. ISBN 0-434-14824-5*
    Pan, 1987. (pbk). ISBN 0-330-29964-6*

1987

    Peter Benson
    The levels
    Constable, 1987. ISBN 0-09-467680-1*
    Penguin, 1988. (pbk). ISBN 0-14-010635-9*

1988

    Lucy Ellman
    Sweet desserts
    Virago, 1988. ISBN 0-86068-847-X*

23 Hawthornden Prize

The prize, one of the the oldest along with the James Tait Black Memorial Prize, was founded by Alice Warrender to encourage what the trustees describe as 'imaginative literature' (which can include non-fiction works) by authors under 41. The prize of £750 and a silver medal is awarded annually.

Contact

Hawthornden Trust
Hawthornden Castle
Lasswade
Midlothian
Scotland
Tel. (031) 440 2180

1919

Edward Shanks
Queen of China and other poems
Martin Secker, 1919

1920

John Freeman
Poems old and new
Selwyn & Blount, 1920

1921

Romer Wilson
The death of society
Collins, 1921

1922

Edmund Blunden
The shepherd and other poems of peace and war
Richard Cobden-Sanderson, 1922

1923

David Garnett
Lady into fox
Chatto & Windus, 1922
Hogarth Press, 1985. (pbk).
ISBN 0-7012-1923-8*

1924

Ralph Hale Mottram
The Spanish farm
Chatto & Windus, 1924

1925

Sean O'Casey
Juno and the paycock
French, 1924
French, 1968. (pbk). ISBN 0-573-01214-8*
Macmillan Educational, 1988. (pbk).
ISBN 0-333-46585-7*

1926

Victoria Sackville-West
The land: A poem
Heinemann, 1926

1927

Henry Williamson
Tarka the otter
Webb & Bower, new ed. 1985.
ISBN 0-86350-074-9*
Ulverscroft Large Print Books, 1981.
ISBN 0-7089-0545-5*
Macmillan Educational, 1981. (pbk).
ISBN 0-333-30602-3*
Penguin, 1971. (pbk). ISBN 0-14-030060-0*
Penguin, 1985. (pbk). ISBN 0-14-059011-0*

1928

Siegfried Sassoon
Memoirs of a fox hunting man
Faber & Faber, 1928
Faber & Faber, 1964. (pbk).
ISBN 0-571-06454-X*

1929

Lord David Cecil
The stricken deer: William Cowper
Constable, 1988. (pbk). ISBN 0-09-468430-8*

1930

Geoffrey Dennis
The end of the world
Eyre & Spottiswoode, 1930

1931

Kate O'Brien
Without my cloak
Heinemann, 1931
Virago, 1986. (pbk). ISBN 0-86068-760-0*

1932

Charles Morgan
The fountain
Robson Books, new ed. 1988.
ISBN 0-86051-513-3*
Robson Books, new ed. 1988. (pbk).
ISBN 0-86051-514-1*

1933

Victoria Sackville-West
Collected poems
L. & V. Woolf, 1933

1934

James Hilton
Lost horizon
Macmillan, 1933. ISBN 0-333-05243-9*
Ulverscroft Large Print Books, 1984.
ISBN 0-7089-8170-4*
Macmillan, 1954. (pbk). ISBN 0-333-43270-3*

1935

Robert Graves
I Claudius
Methuen, 1976. ISBN 0-413-37070-4*
Penguin, 1969. (pbk). ISBN 0-14-000318-5*

1936

Evelyn Waugh
Edmund Campion: Scholar, priest, hero and martyr
Cassell, 1987. ISBN 0-304-31434-X*

1937

Ruth Pitter
A trophy of arms: Poems 1926–1935
Cresset Press, 1936

Hawthornden Prize

1938
    David Michael Jones
    In parenthesis
    Faber & Faber, 1937. ISBN 0-571-05661-X*

1939
    Christopher Hassall
    Penthesperon
    Heinemann, 1938

1940
    James Pope-Hennessy
    London fabric
    Batsford, 1939

1941
    Graham Greene
    The power the glory
    Bodley Head, new ed. 1971.
    ISBN 0-370-01442-1*
    Heinemann, new ed. 1971. ISBN 0-434-30556-1*
    Heinemann Educational, 1963. (pbk).
    ISBN 0-435-17350-2*
    Penguin, 1969. (pbk). ISBN 0-14-001791-7*

1942
    John Llewellyn Rhys
    England is my village
    Faber & Faber, 1941

1943
    Sidney Keyes
    The cruel solstice and the iron laurel
    Routledge, 1943

1944
    Martyn Skinner
    Letters to Malaya
    Puttnam, 1944

1945 – 57   No Awards

1958
    Dom Moraes
    A beginning
    Parton Press, 1958. BNB B58-8801

Hawthornden Prize

1959 No Award

1960
Alan Sillitoe
The loneliness of the long-distance runner
W. H. Allen, 1959. BNB B59-12957
Granada, 1985. (pbk). ISBN 0-586-06503-2*
Hutchinson Educational, 1983. (pbk).
ISBN 0-09-152201-3*

1961
Ted Hughes
Lupercal
Faber & Faber, 1960. BNB B60-03885
Faber & Faber, 1970. (pbk).
ISBN 0-571-09246-2*

1962
Robert Shaw
The sun doctor
Chatto & Windus, 1961. BNB B61-10531

1963
Alistair Horne
The price of glory: Verdun 1916
Macmillan, 1962. BNB B62-17525
Penguin, 1964. (pbk). ISBN 0-14-002215-5*

1964
V. S. Naipaul
Mr Stone and the knight's companions
Deutsch, 1963. BNB B63-07802
Penguin, 1977. (pbk). ISBN 0-14-003712-8*

1965
William Trevor
The old boys
Bodley Head, 1975. ISBN 0-370-10591-5*

1966 No Award

1967

Michael Frayn
The Russian interpreter
Collins, 1966. BNB B66-06163
Fontana, 1985. (pbk). ISBN 0-00-654053-8*

1968

Michael Levey
Early Renaissance
Penguin, 1967. (pbk). BNB B67-25461*

1969

Geoffrey Hill
King Log
Deutsch, 1968. ISBN 0-233-96021-X

1970

Piers Paul Read
Monk Dawson
Secker & Warburg, 1969. ISBN 0-436-40971-2*

1971–73

No Awards

1974

Oliver Sacks
Awakenings
Duckworth, 1973. ISBN 0-7156-0709-X
Pan, 1983. (pbk). ISBN 0-330-26924-0*

1975

David Lodge
Changing places
Secker & Warburg, 1975. ISBN 0-436-25660-6*
Chivers Press, 1986. (large print ed.).
ISBN 0-7451-7012-9*
Penguin, 1978. (pbk). ISBN 0-14-004656-9*

1976

Robert Nye
Falstaff: Being the 'Acta domini Johannis Fastolfe', or, 'Life and valiant deeds of Sir John Faustoff', or 'The Hundred Days War'
Hamish Hamilton, 1976. ISBN 0-241-89429-8

Hawthornden Prize

1977
Bruce Chatwin
In Patagonia
Cape, 1982. ISBN 0-224-01419-6*
Pan, 1979. (pbk). ISBN 0-330-25644-0*

1978
David Cook
Walter
Secker & Warburg, 1978. ISBN 0-436-10672-8*
Arrow, 1988. (pbk). ISBN 0-09-955650-8*

1979
P. S. Rushforth
Kindergarten
Hamish Hamilton, 1979. ISBN 0-241-10263-4

1980
Christopher Reid
Arcadia
Oxford University Press, 1979. (pbk).
ISBN 0-19-211889-7*

1981
Douglas Dunn
St Kilda's Parliament
Faber & Faber, 1981. ISBN 0-571-11770-8

1982
Timothy Mo
Sour sweet
Deutsch, 1982. ISBN 0-233-97365-6*
Sphere, 1983. (pbk). ISBN 0-349-12392-6*

1983
Jonathan Keates
Allegro postillions
Salamander, 1983. ISBN 0-907540-36-8*

1984 – 87 No Awards

1988
Paul Theroux
Riding the iron rooster: By train through China
Hamish Hamilton, 1988. ISBN 0-241-12547-2*

1989
Alan Bennett
Talking heads
BBC, 1988. (pbk). ISBN 0-563-20622-5*

24 David Higham Prize for Fiction

The prize, of £1,000, was inaugurated in 1975 to mark the late David Higham's 80th birthday and is awarded annually to a citizen of Britain, the Commonwealth, Republic of Ireland, Pakistan or South Africa for a first novel or book of short stories.

Contact   Book Trust
Book House
45 East Hill
London SW18 2QZ
Tel. 01-870 9055/8

1975

Jane Gardam
Black faces, white faces
Hamish Hamilton, 1975. ISBN 0-241-89250-3*
Sphere, 1982. (pbk). ISBN 0-349-11407-2*

Matthew Vaughan
Chalky
Secker & Warburg, 1975. ISBN 0-436-55260-4

1976

Caroline Blackwood
The stepdaughter
Duckworth, 1976. ISBN 0-7156-0967-X

1977

Patricia Finney
A shadow of gulls
Collins, 1977. ISBN 0-00-222137-3

1978

Leslie Norris
Sliding
Dent, 1978. ISBN 0-460-12038-7*
Longman, 1981. (pbk). ISBN 0-582-22066-1*

David Higham Prize for Fiction

1979
>
> **John Harvey**
> *The plate shop*
> Collins, 1979. ISBN 0-00-221676-0

1980
>
> **Ted Harriot**
> *Keep on running*
> Secker & Warburg, 1980. ISBN 0-436-19118-0

1981
>
> **Christopher Hope**
> *A separate development*
> Routledge & Kegan Paul, 1981.
> ISBN 0-7100-0954-2*

1982
>
> **Glyn Hughes**
> *Where I used to play on the green*
> Gollancz, 1982. ISBN 0-575-02997-8

1983
>
> **R. M. Lamming**
> *The notebook of Gismonde Cavalletti*
> Cape, 1983. ISBN 0-224-02141-9

1984
>
> **James Buchan**
> *A parish of rich women*
> Hamish Hamilton, 1984. ISBN 0-241-11310-5*
> Futura, 1987. (pbk). ISBN 0-7088-3370-5*

1985
>
> **Patricia Ferguson**
> *Family myths and legends*
> Deutsch, 1985. ISBN 0-233-97726-0*
> Penguin, 1986. (pbk). ISBN 0-14-008376-6*

1986
>
> **Jim Crace**
> *Continent*
> Heinemann, 1986. (pbk). ISBN 0-434-14824-5*
> Pan, 1987. (pbk). ISBN 0-330-29964-6*

David Higham Prize for Fiction

1987

    Adam Zameenzad
The thirteenth house
Fourth Estate, 1987. ISBN 0-947795-56-1*
Fontana, 1988. (pbk). ISBN 0-00-654333-2*

1988

    Carol Birch
Life in the palace
Macmillan, 1988. ISBN 0-333-46034-0*

25 The Historical Novel Prize in Memory of Georgette Heyer

The prize, of £5,000, is awarded annually by the Heyer Estate in memory of the late Georgette Heyer for an outstanding historical (set before 1939) novel.

Contact
The Bodley Head
32 Bedford Square
London WC1B 3EL
Tel. 01-631 4434

or
Corgi Books
Century House
61 – 63 Uxbridge Road
London W5 5SA
Tel. 01-579 2652

1978

Rhona Martin
Gallows wedding
Bodley Head, 1978. ISBN 0-370-30109-9*

1979

Norah Lofts
The day of the butterfly
Bodley Head, 1979. ISBN 0-370-30200-1
Ulverscroft Large Print Books, 1981.
ISBN 0-7089-0623-0*

1980

Lynn Guest
Children of Hachiman
Bodley Head, 1980. ISBN 0-370-30311-3

1981

Valerie Fitzgerald
Zemindar
Bodley Head, 1981. ISBN 0-370-30429-2*

1982
No Award

Historical Novel Prize

1983

    Kathleen Herbert
Queen of the lightning
Bodley Head, 1983. ISBN 0-370-30536-1*

1984

    Alan Fisher
The Terioki crossing
Bodley Head, 1984. ISBN 0-370-30609-0
Ulverscroft Large Print Books, 1985.
ISBN 0-7089-8283-2*

1985

    Susan Kay
Legacy
Bodley Head, 1985. ISBN 0-370-30874-3*
Corgi, 1936. (pbk). ISBN 0-552-12720-5*

1986

    Michael Weston
The cage
Bodley Head, 1986. ISBN 0-370-30883-2*
Ulverscroft Large Print Books, 1987.
ISBN 0-7089-8383-9*

1987

    Patricia Wright
I am England
Bodley Head, 1987. ISBN 0-370-31083-7*
Ulverscroft Large Print Books, 1988.
ISBN 0-7089-8491-6*
Corgi, 1988. (pbk). ISBN 0-552-13290-X*

1988   No Award

26 Winifred Holtby Memorial Prize

In 1966 Vera Brittain gave to the Royal Society of Literature a sum of money to provide an annual prize in honour of Winifred Holtby. The prize, of £500, is for the best regional novel or non-fiction work concerning a regional subject.

Contact The Royal Society of Literature
1 Hyde Park Gardens
London W2 2LT
Tel. 01-723 5104

1975

Jane Gardam
Black faces, white faces
Hamish Hamilton, 1975. ISBN 0-241-89250-3*
Sphere, 1982. (pbk). ISBN 0-349-11407-2*

1976

Eugene McCabe
Victims
Gollancz, 1976. ISBN 0-575-02169-1

1977

Anita Desai
Fire on the mountain
Heinemann, 1977. ISBN 0-434-18631-7*
Penguin, 1981. (pbk). ISBN 0-14-005347-6*

1978

Richard Herley
The stone arrow
Peter Davies, 1978. ISBN 0-432-06675-6

1979 No Award

1980

Elsa Joubert
Poppie
Hodder & Stoughton, 1981. (pbk).
ISBN 0-340-27269-4*

Winifred Holtby Memorial Prize

1981

Alan Judd
A breed of horses
Hodder & Stoughton, 1981.
ISBN 0-340-26334-2*
Magna Print Books, 1986. (large print ed.).
ISBN 0-86009-950-4*
Magna Print Books, 1986. (large print ed, pbk.).
ISBN 0-86009-951-2*
Fontana, 1982. (pbk). ISBN 0-00-616458-7*

1982

Kazuo Ishiguro
A pale view of the hills
Faber & Faber, 1982. ISBN 0-571-11866-6
Penguin, 1983. (pbk). ISBN 0-14-006260-2*

1983

Graham Swift
Waterland
Heinemann, 1983. ISBN 0-434-75330-0*
Chivers Press, 1984. (large print ed.).
ISBN 0-86220-114-4*
Pan, 1984. (pbk). ISBN 0-330-28395-2*

1984

Balraj Khanna
A nation of fools: Scenes from Indian life
Michael Joseph, 1983. ISBN 0-7181-2387-5

1985   No Award

1986

Maggie Hemingway
The bridge
Cape, 1986. ISBN 0-224-02832-4*
Chivers Press, 1988. (large print ed.).
ISBN 0-7451-0696-X*
Pan, 1987. (pbk). ISBN 0-330-29715-5*

1987   No Award

27 Nelson Hurst and Marsh Biography Award

A biennial award of £2,000 for a significant biography.

Contact The Author's Club
40 Dover Street
London W1X 3RB
Tel. 01-499 8581

1987

Roland Huntford
Shackleton
Hodder & Stoughton, 1985.
ISBN 0-340-25007-0*

28 Sir Peter Kent Conservation Book Prize

Established in 1987 to reward and stimulate conservation writing in memory of the distinguished geologist and environmentalist. The prize of £1,500 is sponsored by BP Exploration with the support of the Nature Conservancy Council.

Contact   Book Trust
               Book House
               45 East Hill
               London SW18 2QZ
               Tel. 01-870 9055

1987
               Chris Baines
               The wild side of town
               BBC, 1986. ISBN 0-563-21312-4*
               BBC, 1986. (pbk). ISBN 0-563-21309-4*

1988/89
               Jeremy Purseglove
               Taming the flood: History and natural history of rivers and wetlands
               Oxford University Press, 1988.
               ISBN 0-19-215891-0*

29 King George's Fund for Sailors Book of the Sea Award

A prize of £1,000 and £250 Merit Award for the best non-fiction book which contributes to the knowledge or enjoyment of those who love the sea.

Contact King George's Fund for Sailors
1 Chesham Street
London SW1X 8NF
Tel. 01-235 2884

1970

John Leather
The gaff rig
Adlard Coles, 1970. ISBN 0-229-94789-9*
Grafton, 2nd ed. 1989. (pbk).
ISBN 0-229-11844-5*

1971

Eric Tabarly
Pen Duick
Coles, 1971. ISBN 0-229-98647-1

1972

Richard Hough
Captain Bligh and Mr Christian: The men and the mutiny
Hutchinson, 1972. ISBN 0-09-112860-9
Cresset Library, 1988. (pbk).
ISBN 0-09-182328-5*

1973

David Macgregor
Fast sailing ships: Their design and construction, 1775–1875
New ed. Conway Maritime Press, 1988.
ISBN 0-85177-452-0*

King George's Fund for Sailors Book of the Sea Award

1974
    H. R. Oram
    Ready for sea
    Seeley, 1974. ISBN 0-85422-082-8

1975   No Award

1976
    Joyce D. Sleightholme
    This is sailboat cruising
    Nautical Publishing, 1976. ISBN 0-245-52567-X

1977
    Dudley Pope
    Harry Morgan's way: Biography of Sir Henry Morgan, 1635 – 84
    Secker & Warburg, 1977. ISBN 0-436-37735-7*

1978
    Tim Severin
    The Brendan voyage
    Hutchinson, 1978. ISBN 0-09-133100-5
    Isis Large Print Books, 1987.
    ISBN 0-85089-162-1*

1979 – 1980   No Award

1981
    Richard England
    Schoonerman
    Bodley Head, 1981. ISBN 0-370-30377-6

1982
    Tim Severin
    The Sinbad voyage
    Hutchinson, 1982. ISBN 0-09-150560-7
    Magna Print Books, 1986. (large print ed.).
    ISBN 0-86009-754-4*

1983
    Dan van der Vat
    The last corsair: Story of the Emden
    Hodder & Stoughton, 1983.
    ISBN 0-340-23245-0*
    Granada, 1984. (pbk). ISBN 0-586-06265-3*

King George's Fund for Sailors Book of the Sea Award

1984

                Bob Fisher
                The great yacht races
                Orbis, 1984. ISBN 0-85613-683-2

merit award   **Peter Cremer**
                U333: Story of a U-boat ace
                Bodley Head, 1984. ISBN 0-370-30545-0
                Grafton, 1986. (pbk). ISBN 0-586-06294-7

1985

                Paul Heiney and Libby Purves
                Sailing weekend book
                Nautical Books, 1985. ISBN 0-85177-346-X*

merit prize   **Cornelius van Rietschoten and Barry Pickthall**
                Blue water sailing
                Nautical Books, 1985. ISBN 0-85177-344-3*

1986

                Nigel Calder
                The English Channel
                Chatto & Windus, 1986. ISBN 0-7011-3053-9*

merit prize   **Jonathan Raban**
                Coasting
                Collins Harvill, 1986. ISBN 0-00-272119-8*
                Pan, 1987. (pbk). ISBN 0-330-29977-8*

1987

                Naomi James
                Courage at sea
                Stanley Paul, 1987. ISBN 0-09-171250-5*

merit prize   **John Wells**
                The immortal warrior
                Mason, 1987. ISBN 0-85937-333-9

1988

                Tom Cunliffe
                Topsail and battleaxe
                David and Charles, 1988. ISBN 0-7153-9123-2*

King George's Fund for Sailors Book of the Sea Award

merit prize **Frank Welsh**
Building the trireme
Constable, 1988. ISBN 0-09-466880-9*

30 London Tourist Board Guide Book of the Year Awards

The awards, each a gift and trophy for the author and certificate for the publisher, are for the best general and the best specialist guide books on London.

Contact Public Relations Manager
London Tourist Board
26 Grosvenor Gardens
London SW1W 0DU
Tel. 01-730 3450

1985
general

Chris Turner
London step by step
Pan, 1985. (pbk). ISBN 0-330-28814-8*
Pan, 1988. (pbk). ISBN 0-330-30476-3*

specialist

Richard Trench and Ellis Hillman
London under London: A subterranean guide
John Murray, 1987. ISBN 0-7195-4080-1
John Murray, 1988. (pbk). ISBN 0-7195-4617-6*

1986
general

Ilva French (ed.)
Blue guide to London
13th ed. A. & C. Black, 1986. (pbk).
ISBN 0-7136-3083-3*

specialist

Christopher Simon Sykes
Private palaces: Life in the Greater London houses
Chatto & Windus, 1985. ISBN 0-7011-3001-6*

1987
general

R. Wurman
Access travel guide to London
Simon & Schuster, 1987. ISBN 0-671-62576-4*

LTB Guide Book of the Year Awards

specialist **Guiseppi Scimone and Michael Levey**
London museums and collections
2nd ed. A. & C. Black, 1986. (pbk).
ISBN 0-7136-2784-0

1988
general **Louise Nicolson**
Definitive guide to London
Bodley Head, 1988. ISBN 0-370-31032-2*

specialist **Mark Edmonds**
Inside Soho
Robert Nicholson, 1988. ISBN 0-948576-12-X*

31 Roger Machell Prize

Sponsored by Hamish Hamilton the prize, of £2,000, is awarded for a non-fiction work on any of the performing arts.

Contact The Society of Authors
84 Drayton Gardens
London SW10 9SB
Tel. 01-373 6642

1986

David Robinson
Chaplin: His life and art
Collins, 1985. ISBN 0-00-216387-X*
Grafton, 1986. (pbk). ISBN 0-586-08544-0*

1987

Ian Bevan and Kurt Ganzl
The British musical theatre
Macmillan, 1986. ISBN 0-333-41954-5*
Vol. 1. Macmillan, 1988. (pbk).
ISBN 0-333-39839-4*
Vol. 2. Macmillan, 1988. (pbk).
ISBN 0-333-39744-4*

1988

Peter Conrad
A song of love and death: The meaning of opera
Chatto & Windus, 1987. ISBN 0-7011-3274-4*

32 Mackenzie Prize

The prize is awarded by a selection committee of three senior British political scientists to the best book published each year on any aspect of political science.

Contact Political Studies Association
School of Social Sciences and Business
Polytechnic of Central London
70 Great Portland Street
London W1

1986

Joseph Raz
The morality of freedom
Clarendon Press, 1986. ISBN 0-19-824772-9
Oxford University Press, 1988. (pbk).
ISBN 0-19-824807-5*

1987

W. H. Greenleaf
British political tradition. Vol. 3: A much governed nation
Part 1. Methuen, 1987. ISBN 0-416-36820-4*
Part 2. Methuen, 1987. ISBN 0-416-02152-2*

33 McVitie's Prize for the Scottish Writer of the Year

An annual prize of £5,000, open to writers, in any field of literature, born in Scotland or who have been resident in Scotland, or who take Scotland as their inspiration.

Contact   Michael Kelly Associates Ltd
65 Bath Street
Glasgow G2 2BX
Tel. (041) 333 9711

1987

David Thomson
Nairn in darkness and light
Hutchinson, 1987. ISBN 0-09-168360-2*
Arrow, 1988. (pbk). ISBN 0-09-959990-2*

1988

Bernard Maclaverty
Great Profundo: And other stories
Cape, 1987. ISBN 0-224-02483-3*

Edwin Mickleburgh
Beyond the frozen sea: Visions of Antarctica
Bodley Head, 1987. ISBN 0-370-31027-6*

34 Somerset Maugham Award

Founded in 1946 by the late Somerset Maugham to encourage young writers to travel abroad. The award, of £3,000 – £4,000, is for a work by an author under 35.

Contact Society of Authors
84 Drayton Gardens
London SW10 9SB
Tel. 01-373 6642

1947
A. L. Barker
Innocents
Hogarth Press, 1947

1948
P. H. Newby
Journey to the interior
Cape, 1945

1949
Hamish Henderson
Elegies for the dead in Cyrenaica
John Lehmann, 1948

1950
Nigel Kneale
Tomato Cain and other stories
Collins, 1949

1951
Roland Camberton
Scamp
Lehmann, 1950. BNB B50-10208

1952
Francis King
The dividing stream
Longmans Green, 1951. BNB B51-06774

Somerset Maugham Award

1953

Emyr Humphries
Hear and forgive
Gollancz, 1952. BNB B52-11836

1954

Doris Lessing
Five: Short novels
Michael Joseph, 1953. BNB B53-07932
Panther, 1969. (pbk). ISBN 0-586-02876-5*

1955

Kingsley Amis
Lucky Jim
Gollancz, new ed. 1984. ISBN 0-575-03484-X*
Longman, 1963. (pbk). ISBN 0-582-53020-2*
Penguin, 1970. (pbk). ISBN 0-14-001648-1*

1956

Elizabeth Jennings
A way of looking: Poems
Deutsch, 1955. BNB B55-16510

1957

George Lamming
In the castle of my skin
Michael Joseph, 1953. BNB B53-03220
Longman, 1979. (pbk). ISBN 0-582-64267-1*

1958

John Wain
Preliminary essays
Macmillan, 1957. BNB B57-11555

1959

Thom Gunn
A sense of movement
Faber & Faber, 1957. BNB B57-08176
Faber & Faber, 1968. (pbk).
ISBN 0-571-08530-X*

Somerset Maugham Award

1960

Ted Hughes
The hawk in the rain
Faber & Faber, 1957. BNB B57-13174
Faber & Faber, 1968. (pbk).
ISBN 0-571-08614-4*

1961

V. S. Naipaul
Miguel Street
World Distributors, 1960. BNB B60-14976
Heinemann Educational, 1975.
ISBN 0-435-98645-7*
Penguin, 1971. (pbk). ISBN 0-14-003302-5*

1962

Hugh Thomas
The Spanish Civil War
Hamish Hamilton, 2nd ed. 1977.
ISBN 0-241-89450-6*
Rev. ed. Penguin, 1965. (pbk).
ISBN 0-14-020970-0*

1963

David Storey
Flight into Camden
Cape, new ed. 1982. ISBN 0-224-02033-1*

1964

Dan Jacobson
Time of arrival: And other essays
Weidenfeld & Nicolson, 1963. BNB B63-03845

John le Carré
The spy who came in from the cold
Gollancz, 1963. ISBN 0-575-02900-5
Hutchinson Educational, 1966.
ISBN 0-09-076870-1*
Hutchinson Educational, 1974. (pbk).
ISBN 0-09-120131-4*
Pan, 1965. (pbk). ISBN 0-330-20107-7*

1965

Peter Everett
Negatives
Cape, 1964. BNB B64-21793

Somerset Maugham Award

1966

Michael Frayn
The tin men
Collins, 1965. BNB B65-01613
Fontana, 1985. (pbk). ISBN 0-00-654102-X*

Julian Mitchell
The white father
Constable, 1964. BNB B64-06030

1967

B. S. Johnson
Trawl
Secker & Warburg, 1966. BNB B66-21822

Andrew Sinclair
The better half: Emancipation of the American woman
Greenwood Press, new ed. 1981.
ISBN 0-313-22828-0*

1968

Paul Bailey
At the Jerusalem
Cape, 1967. BNB B67-10626
Penguin, 1982. (pbk). ISBN 0-14-005796-X*

Seamus Heaney
Death of a naturalist
Faber & Faber, 1966. BNB B66-09171
Faber & Faber, 1969. (pbk).
ISBN 0-571-09024-9*

1969

Angela Carter
Several perceptions
Heinemann, 1968. ISBN 0-434-10953-3

1970

Jane Gaskell
A sweet sweet summer
Hodder & Stoughton, 1969.
ISBN 0-340-11000-7*

Somerset Maugham Award

Piers Paul Read
Monk Dawson
Secker & Warburg, 1969. ISBN 0-436-40971-2*

1971

Susan Hill
I'm the king of the castle
Hamish Hamilton, 1970. ISBN 0-241-01910-9
Heinemann Educational, 1982. (pbk).
ISBN 0-435-27085-0*
Longman, 1981. (pbk). ISBN 0-582-22173-0*
Penguin, 1974. (pbk). ISBN 0-14-003491-8*

Richard William Barber
The knight and chivalry
Boydell Press, 2nd ed. 1974.
ISBN 0-85115-041-1

Michael Hastings
Tussy is me
Weidenfeld & Nicolson, 1970.
ISBN 0-297-17774-5

1972

Douglas Dunn
Terry Street
Faber & Faber, 1971. ISBN 0-571-09713-8

Gillian Tindall
Fly away home
Hodder & Stoughton, 1971. ISBN 0-340-15039-4

1973

Peter Prince
Play things
Gollancz, 1972. ISBN 0-575-01500-4

Paul Strathern
A season in Abyssinia: An impersonation
Macmillan, 1972. ISBN 0-333-13420-6

Jonathan Street
Prudence dictates: A comic tale
MacGibbon & Kee, 1972. ISBN 0-261-10007-6

Somerset Maugham Award

1974

    Martin Amis
The Rachel papers
Cape, 1973. ISBN 0-224-00912-5
Penguin, 1984. (pbk). ISBN 0-14-007001-X*

1975   No Award

1976

    Dominic Cooper
The dead of winter
Chatto & Windus, 1975. ISBN 0-7011-2076-2
Faber & Faber, 1985. (pbk).
ISBN 0-571-13601-X*

1977

    Richard Holmes
Shelley: The pursuit
Quartet, 1976. ISBN 0-7043-3111-X*
Penguin, 1987. (pbk). ISBN 0-14-058037-9*

1978

    Tom Paulin
A state of justice
Faber & Faber, 1977. (pbk). ISBN 0-571-10982-9

    Nigel Williams
My life closed twice
Secker & Warburg, 1977. ISBN 0-436-57154-4*
Faber & Faber, 1986. (pbk).
ISBN 0-571-14572-8*

1979

    Helen Hodgman
Jack and Jill
Duckworth, 1978. ISBN 0-7156-1304-9
Virago, 1989. (pbk). ISBN 0-85381-023-1*

    Sara Maitland
Daughter of Jerusalem
Blond & Briggs, 1978. ISBN 0-85634-084-7
Pan, 1987. (pbk). ISBN 0-330-29393-1*

Somerset Maugham Award

1980

Max Hastings
Bomber command
Michael Joseph, 1979. ISBN 0-7181-1603-8*
Pan, 1981. (pbk). ISBN 0-330-26236-X*

Christopher Reid
Arcadia
Oxford University Press, 1979. (pbk).
ISBN 0-19-211889-7*

Humphrey Carpenter
The inklings
Allen & Unwin, 1978. ISBN 0-04-809011-5
Unwin, 1981. (pbk). ISBN 0-04-809013-1*

1981

Julian Barnes
Metroland
Cape, 1980. ISBN 0-224-01762-4
Robin Clark, 1981. (pbk).
ISBN 0-86072-048-9*

Clive Sinclair
Hearts of gold
Allison & Busby, 1979. ISBN 0-85031-268-X

A. N. Wilson
The healing art
Secker & Warburg, 1980. ISBN 0-436-57603-1*
Penguin, 1982. (pbk). ISBN 0-14-006122-3*

1982

William Boyd
A good man in Africa
Hamish Hamilton, 1981. ISBN 0-241-10516-1*
Magna Print Books, 1984. (large print ed.)
ISBN 0-86009-584-3*
Penguin, 1982. (pbk). ISBN 0-14-005887-7*

Adam Mars-Jones
Lantern lecture
Faber & Faber, 1981. ISBN 0-571-11813-5*
Pan, 1982. (pbk). ISBN 0-330-26805-8*

1983

Lisa St Aubin de Terán
Keepers of the house
Cape, 1982. ISBN 0-224-02001-3*
Penguin, 1983. (pbk). ISBN 0-14-006372-2*

1984

Peter Ackroyd
The last testament of Oscar Wilde
Hamish Hamilton, 1983. ISBN 0-241-10964-7*
Sphere, 1984. (pbk). ISBN 0-349-10059-4*

Timothy Garton Ash
The Polish revolution: Solidarity, 1980–82
Cape, 1983. ISBN 0-224-02042-0*

Sean O'Brien
The indoor park
Bloodaxe, 1983. ISBN 1-85224-013-X*

1985

Blake Morrison
Dark glasses
Chatto & Windus, 1984. (pbk).
ISBN 0-7011-2875-5*

Jeremy Reed
By the fisheries
Cape, 1984. (pbk). ISBN 0-224-02154-0*

Jane Rogers
Her living image
Faber & Faber, 1984. ISBN 0-571-14772-0*
Fontana, 1986. (pbk). ISBN 0-00-654144-5*

1986

Patricia Ferguson
Family myths and legends
Deutsch, 1985. ISBN 0-233-97726-0*
Penguin, 1986. (pbk). ISBN 0-14-008376-6*

Adam Nicolson
Frontiers
Weidenfeld & Nicolson, 1985.
ISBN 0-297-78709-8

Somerset Maugham Award

Tim Parks
Tongues of flame
Heinemann, 1985. ISBN 0-434-57735-9*
Fontana, 1986. (pbk). ISBN 0-00-617333-0*

1987

Stephen Gregory
The cormorant
Heinemann, 1986. ISBN 0-434-30576-6*
Sceptre, 1987. (pbk). ISBN 0-340-41690-4*

Janni Howker
Isaac Campion
Julia Macrae, 1985. ISBN 0-86203-194-X*
Armada Books, 1987. (pbk).
ISBN 0-00-672790-5*
Heinemann Educational, 1988. (pbk).
ISBN 0-435-12326-2*

Andrew Motion
The Lamberts: George, Constant and Kit
Chatto & Windus, 1986. ISBN 0-7011-2731-7*
Hogarth Press, 1987. (pbk).
ISBN 0-7012-0799-X*

1988

Jimmy Burns
The land that lost its heroes: Falklands, the post-war and Alfonsin
Bloomsbury, 1987. ISBN 0-7475-0002-9*
Bloomsbury, 1987. (pbk). ISBN 0-7475-0111-4*

Carol Ann Duffy
Selling Manhattan
Anvil Press, 1987. (pbk). ISBN 0-85646-194-6*

Matthew Kneale
Whore banquets
Gollancz, 1987. ISBN 0-575-03921-3*
Dent, 1988. (pbk). ISBN 0-460-12553-2*

1989

Rupert Christiansen
Romantic affinities: Portraits from an age, 1780–1830
Bodley Head, 1988. ISBN 0-370-31117-5*
Sphere, 1989. (pbk). ISBN 0-7474-0404-6*

Somerset Maugham Award

Alan Hollinghurst
The swimming pool library
Chatto & Windus, 1988.
ISBN 0-7011-3282-5*
Penguin, 1989. (pbk). ISBN 0-14-011610-9*

Diedre Madden
the birds of the innocent wood
Faber & Faber, 1988. ISBN 0-571-14880-8*
Faber & Faber, 1989. (pbk).
ISBN 0-571-15281-3*

35 MIND Book of the Year

Founded in memory of Allen Lane and supported by the Allen Lane Foundation, the award, of £1,000, is presented to the author of a work which makes the greatest contribution to public understanding of mental illness or mental handicap.

Contact   MIND
22 Harley Street
London W1N 2ED
Tel. 01-637 0741

1981

Sheila Macleod
The art of starvation: An adolescent observed
Virago, 1981. ISBN 0-86068-164-5
Virago, 1981. (pbk). ISBN 0-86068-196-6*

1982

Rosemary Crossley and Anne McDonald
Annie's coming out
Penguin, 1982. (pbk). ISBN 0-14-022443-2

1983

Dorothy Rowe
Depression: The way out of your prison
Routledge & Kegan Paul, 1983.
ISBN 0-7100-9699-2*

1984

Edward Adamson
Art as healing
Coventure, 1984. (pbk). ISBN 0-904575-24-1*

1985

Audrey Peckham
A woman in custody
Fontana, 1985. (pbk). ISBN 0-00-636952-9*

1986
Lindsay Knight
Talking to a stranger: A consumer's guide to therapy
Fontana, 1986. (pbk). ISBN 0-00-636780-1*

1987
Miriam Hastings
The Minator hunt: A novel
Harvester Press, 1987. ISBN 0-7108-1200-0*

1988
J. Bernlef
Out of mind
Faber & Faber, 1988. ISBN 0-571-14954-3*

36 NCR Book Award for Non-Fiction

Sponsored by NCR Limited, this is now the UK's most valuable literary award with £25,000 for the winner and £1,500 to the shortlisted authors. The aim of the award is to stimulate interest in non-fiction writing, publishing and reading. Open to writers from the British Commonwealth and the Republic of Ireland.

Contact   NCR Ltd
206 Marylebone Road
London NW1 6LY
Tel. 01-725 8246

1988

David Thomson
Nairn in darkness and light
Hutchinson, 1987. ISBN 0-09-168360-2*
Arrow, 1988. (pbk). ISBN 0-09-959990-2*

shortlist

Nirad C. Chaudhuri
Thy hand, Great Anarch!: India 1921–1952
Chatto & Windus, 1987. ISBN 0-7011-2476-8*

Max Hastings
The Korean War
Michael Joseph, 1987. ISBN 0-7181-1603-8*
Pan, 1988. (pbk). ISBN 0-330-30265-5*

Michael Ignatieff
The Russian album
Chatto & Windus, 1987. ISBN 0-7011-3109-8*
Penguin, 1988. (pbk). ISBN 0-14-008808-3*

Claire Tomalin
Katherine Mansfield: A secret life
Viking, 1987. ISBN 0-670-81392-3*
Penguin, 1988. (pbk). ISBN 0-14-011715-6*

NCR Book Award for Non-Fiction

Kathleen Tynan
The life of Kenneth Tynan
Weidenfeld & Nicolson, 1987.
ISBN 0-297-79082-X*
Methuen, 1988. (pbk). ISBN 0-413-18590-7*

1989

Joe Simpson
Touching the void
Cape, 1988. ISBN 0-224-02545-7*
Pan, 1989. (pbk). ISBN 0-330-30859-9*

shortlist

Malcolm Brown and Julia Cave
A touch of genius: The life of T. E. Lawrence
Dent, 1988. ISBN 0-460-04734-5*

Stephen Hawking
A brief history of time
Bantam Press, 1988. ISBN 0-593-01518-5*

A. N. Wilson
Tolstoy
Hamish Hamilton, 1988. ISBN 0-241-12190-6*

37 Odd Fellows (Manchester Unity) Social Concern Book Award

Instituted in 1977 to focus on problems of social concern to the community. The award, of £2,000, is for a book or pamphlet of not fewer than 10,000 words on a specified theme. Authors must be citizens of the Commonwealth, the Republic of Ireland or South Africa or Pakistan.

Contact	Book Trust Book House 45 East Hill London SW18 2QZ Tel. 01-870 9055

1977
old age

Valarie Karn
Retiring to the seaside
Routledge & Kegan Paul, 1977.
ISBN 0-7100-8418-8

Susan Hooker
Caring for elderly people: Understanding and practical help
2nd ed. Routledge & Kegan Paul, 1981. (pbk).
ISBN 0-7100-0890-2*

1978
unemployment

Ruth Lister and Frank Field
Wasted labour: Call for action on unemployment
Child Poverty Action Group, 1978. (pbk).
ISBN 0-903963-58-2*

unexpectant teenager

Gill Brason
The ungreen park
Bodley Head, 1978. ISBN 0-370-30088-2

Odd Fellows Social Concern Book Award

1979
child health — **Merren Parker and David Mauger**
Children with cancer: A handbook for parents and helpers
Cassell, 1979. ISBN 0-304-30237-6*

vandalism — **Michael Rutter** (et al.)
Fifteen thousand hours: Secondary schools and their effect on children
Open Books, 1979. (pbk). ISBN 0-7291-0113-4*

1980
enforced leisure — **Christopher Evans**
The mighty micro: The impact of the computer revolution
Gollancz, 1979. ISBN 0-575-02708-8

employment and the disabled — **Corbet Woodall**
A disjointed life
Heinemann, 1980. ISBN 0-434-87795-6
John Clare, 1982. (pbk). ISBN 0-906549-28-0*

1981
Year of the Disabled

first prize — **Allan T. Sutherland**
Disabled we stand
Souvenir Press, 1981. (pbk).
ISBN 0-285-64937-X*

second prize — **Sarah Boston** (et al.)
Will, my son: The life and death of a mongol child
Free Association Books, 1987. (pbk).
ISBN 0-946960-92-5*
Pluto Press, 1981. (pbk). ISBN 0-86104-346-4*

1982
effects of technology on employment — **Giles Merritt**
World out of work
Collins, 1982. (pbk). ISBN 0-00-216634-8*

Odd Fellows Social Concern Book Award

Eric Arnold (et al.)
Microelectronics and women's employment in Britain
Science Policy Research Unit, Women and Technology Studies, University of Sussex, 1982.
ISBN 0-903622-18-1

1983
children, their welfare and development

Bernard Knight
Sudden death in infancy: The 'cot death' syndrome
Faber & Faber, 1983. ISBN 0-571-13066-6

1984
children in trouble

Ruth Porter
Child sexual abuse within the family
Tavistock, 1984. ISBN 0-422-79280-2
Tavistock, 1984. (pbk). ISBN 0-422-79290-X*

Philippa Russell
The wheelchair child
2nd ed. Souvenir Press, 1984.
ISBN 0-285-64982-5*

John Burnett
Destiny obscure: The autobiography of childhood, education and family from the 1820s to the 1920s
Allen Lane, 1982. ISBN 0-7139-1214-6

1985
uses of voluntary and enforced leisure

Michael Moynagh
Making unemployment work
Lion Publishing, 1985. ISBN 0-85648-849-6*

1986
poverty amid prosperity

Alan McDonald
The Weller way: The story of the Weller Streets Housing Co-operative
Faber & Faber, 1986. ISBN 0-571-13963-9

Marjorie Wallace
The silent twins
Chatto & Windus, 1986. ISBN 0-7011-2712-0*

Odd Fellows Social Concern Book Award

1987
violent society **Vivien Stern**
Bricks of shame: Britain's prisons
Penguin, 1989. (pbk). ISBN 0-14-022864-0*

1988
caring in **Tessa Lorant Warburg**
the community *A voice at twilight: Diary of a dying man*
Peter Owen, 1988. ISBN 0-7026-0706-X*

38 The Portico Prize

A prize of £1,500 for a work set in the north west of England.

Contact The Portico Library
57 Mosley Street
Manchester M2 3HY
Tel. (061) 236 6785

1985

Gary Messinger
Manchester in the Victorian Age: The half-known city
Manchester University Press, 1985.
ISBN 0-7190-1843-9

1986

Don Haworth
Figures in a bygone landscape
Methuen, 1986. ISBN 0-413-42110-4*
Chivers Press, 1989. (large print ed.).
ISBN 0-7451-7155-9*
Methuen, 1987. (pbk). ISBN 0-413-17080-2*

1987

Bill Naughton
On the pig's back
Oxford University Press, 1987.
ISBN 0-19-212257-6*
Oxford University Press, 1988. (pbk).
ISBN 0-19-282141-5*

1988

Margaret Simey
Democracy rediscovered: Study in police accountability
Pluto Press, 1988. ISBN 0-7453-0262-9*

John Stalker
Stalker
Harrap, 1988. ISBN 0-245-54616-2*
Chivers Press, 1988. (large print ed.).
ISBN 0-86220-264-7*
Penguin, 1988. (pbk). ISBN 0-14-011051-8*

39 The John Llewellyn Rhys Memorial Prize

This distinguished prize was founded in 1942 by Jane Oliver in memory of her husband who was killed in active service with the Royal Air Force in 1940. The prize, of £500, sponsored by the Woolwich Building Society, is for a memorable work by a British or Commonwealth author under 35 years old at the time of the book's publication.

Contact Book Trust
Book House
45 East Hill
London SW18 2QZ
Tel. 01-870 9055

1942

Michael Richey
Sunk by a mine
New York Times Magazine, 1942

1943

Morwena Donnelly
Beauty for ashes
Routledge, 1942

1944

Alun Lewis
The last inspection
Allen & Unwin, 1942

1945

James Aldridge
The sea eagle
Michael Joseph, 1944

1946

Oriel Malet
My bird sings
Faber & Faber, 1945

John Llewellyn Rhys Memorial Prize

1947
Anne-Marie Walters
Moondrop to Gascony
Macmillan, 1946

1948
Richard Mason
The wind cannot read
Hodder & Stoughton, 1946
Ulverscroft Large Print Books, 1976.
ISBN 0-85456-435-7*

1949
Emma Smith
Maiden's trip
Putnam, 1948
M. & M. Baldwin, 1987. (pbk).
ISBN 0-947712-05-4*

1950
Kenneth Allsop
Adventure lit their star
Latimer House, 1949

1951
Elizabeth Jane Howard
The beautiful visit
Cape, 1950. BNB B50-03142
Penguin, 1976. (pbk). ISBN 0-14-004139-7*

1952 No Award

1953
Rachel Trickett
The return home
Constable, 1952. BNB B52-09703

1954
Tom Stacey
The hostile sun: A Malayan journey
Duckworth, 1953. BNB B53-15173

1955
John Wiles
The moon to play with
Chatto & Windus, 1954. BNB B54-11541

1956
John Hearne
Voices under the window
Faber & Faber, 1955. BNB B55-11723
Faber & Faber, 1973. (pbk).
ISBN 0-571-09985-8*

1957
Ruskin Bond
The room on the roof
Deutsch, 1956. BNB B56-06166
Penguin, 1988. (pbk). ISBN 0-14-010783-5*

1958
V. S. Naipaul
The mystic masseur
Heinemann, new ed. 1971.
ISBN 0-435-98646-5*
Penguin, 1971. (pbk). ISBN 0-14-002156-6*

1959
Dan Jacobson
A long way to Shiloh
Weidenfeld & Nicolson, 1958. BNB B58-14157

1960
David Caute
At fever pitch
Deutsch, 1959. BNB B59-01668

1961
David Storey
Flight into Camden
Cape, new ed. 1982. ISBN 0-224-02033-1*

1962
Robert Rhodes James
An introduction into the House of Commons
Collins, 1961. BNB B61-19325

John Llewellyn Rhys Memorial Prize

Edward Lucie-Smith
A tropical childhood: And other poems
Oxford University Press, 1961. BNB B61-18636

1963

Peter Marshall
Two lives
Hutchinson, 1962. BNB B62-13291

1964

Nell Dunn
Up the junction
Macgibbon & Kee, 1963. BNB B63-18498
Virago, 1988. (pbk). ISBN 0-86068-989-1*

1965

Julian Mitchell
The white father
Constable, 1964. BNB B64-06030

1966

Margaret Drabble
The millstone
Weidenfeld & Nicolson, 1965.
ISBN 0-297-17881-4*
Penguin, 1969. (pbk). ISBN 0-14-002842-0*

1967

Anthony Masters
The seahorse
Secker & Warburg, 1966. BNB B66-08085

1968

Angela Carter
The magic toyshop
Heinemann, 1967. BNB B67-13542
Virago, 1981. (pbk). ISBN 0-86068-190-4*

1969

Melvyn Bragg
Without a city wall
Secker & Warburg, 1968. ISBN 0-436-06702-1
Sceptre, 1988. (pbk). ISBN 0-340-43102-4*

John Llewellyn Rhys Memorial Prize

1970

    Angus Calder
The People's War: Britain 1939–45
Cape, 1969. ISBN 0-224-61653-6
Grafton, 1979. (pbk). ISBN 0-586-03523-0*

1971

    Shiva Naipaul
Fireflies
Hamish Hamilton, new ed. 1983.
ISBN 0-241-11021-1*
Longman, 1982. (pbk). ISBN 0-582-78538-3*

1972

    Susan Hill
The albatross
Hamish Hamilton, 1972. ISBN 0-241-02258-4
Penguin, 1976. (pbk). ISBN 0-14-004072-2*

1973

    Peter Smalley
A warm gun
Deutsch, 1972. ISBN 0-233-96172-0

1974

    Hugh Fleetwood
The girl who passed for normal
Hamish Hamilton, 1973. ISBN 0-241-02338-6

1975

    David Hare
Knuckle: A play
Faber & Faber, 1974. ISBN 0-571-10467-3
French, 1972. (pbk). ISBN 0-573-01570-8*

    Tim Jeal
Cushing's crusade
Heinemann, 1974. ISBN 0-434-37209-9

1976   No Award

1977
Richard Cork
Vorticism and abstract art in the first machine age
Vol. 1. Gordon Fraser, 1976.
ISBN 0-900406-24-0*
Vol. 2. Gordon Fraser, 1976.
ISBN 0-900406-25-9*

1978
A. N. Wilson
The Sweets of Pimlico
Secker & Warburg, 1977. ISBN 0-436-57600-7*
Penguin, 1983. (pbk). ISBN 0-14-006697-7*

1979
Peter Boardman
The shining mountain: Two men on Changabang's west wall
Hodder & Stoughton, 1978. ISBN 0-340-22375-8

1980
Desmond Hogan
The diamonds at the bottom of the sea: And other stories
Hamish Hamilton, 1979. ISBN 0-341-10123-9

1981
A. N. Wilson
The Laird of Abbotsford: View of Sir Walter Scott
Oxford University Press, 1980.
ISBN 0-19-211756-4*

1982
William Boyd
An ice-cream war
Hamish Hamilton, 1982. ISBN 0-241-10868-3
Penguin, 1983. (pbk). ISBN 0-14-006571-7*

1983
Lisa St Aubin de Terán
The slow train to Milan
Cape, 1983. ISBN 0-224-02077-3*
Penguin, 1984. (pbk). ISBN 0-14-006954-2*

John Llewellyn Rhys Memorial Prize

1984

    Andrew Motion
Dangerous play: Poems 1974–84
Salamander Press, 1984. ISBN 0-907540-46-2*
Penguin, 1985. (pbk). ISBN 0-14-007352-3*

1985

    John Milne
Out of the blue
Hamish Hamilton, 1985. ISBN 0-241-11489-6

1986

    Tim Parks
Loving Roger
Heinemann, 1986. ISBN 0-434-57736-7
Fontana, 1986. (pbk). ISBN 0-00-654236-0*

1987

    Jeannette Winterson
The passion
Bloomsbury Publishing, 1987.
ISBN 0-7475-0034-7*
Penguin, 1988. (pbk). ISBN 0-14-010831-9*

1988

    Matthew Yorke
The March fence
Viking, 1988. ISBN 0-670-81848-8*

40 Romantic Novelists Association Awards

The Association makes two awards a year. The Novel of the Year, £5,000 sponsored by Boots the Chemist, is given to the best romantic novel. From 1976 to 1980 there were two categories, modern and historical. This has now changed and only one award is made regardless of category. The Netta Muskett Award is for the best unpublished romantic novel which has been accepted for publication.

Contact Romantic Novelists Association
20 First Avenue
Amersham
Buckinghamshire HP7 9BJ
Tel. (0494) 727202

1974
novel of the year **Frances Murray**
The burning lamp
Hodder & Stoughton, 1973. ISBN 0-340-17953-8

Netta Muskett **Sheila Walsh**
award *The golden songbird*
Hurst & Blackett, 1975. ISBN 0-09-122180-3
Magna Print Books, 1984. (large print ed.).
ISBN 0-86009-614-9*

1975
novel of the year **Jay Allerton**
Vote for a silk gown
Macdonald & Janes, 1974. ISBN 0-356-08048-X
Ulverscroft Large Print Books, 1986.
ISBN 0-7089-1524-8*

Netta Muskett **Freda Michel**
award *The price of vengeance*
Hale, 1976. ISBN 0-7091-4846-1

1976

novel of the year
historical
Anne Gilbert
The look of innocence
Hodder & Stoughton, 1975. ISBN 0-340-19752-8

modern
Margaret Maddocks
The moon is square
Hurst & Blackett, 1975. ISBN 0-09-124330-0*

Netta Muskett award
Hester Rowan
Overture in Venice
Collins, 1976. ISBN 0-00-233622-7
Ulverscroft Large Print Books, 1985.
ISBN 0-7089-1353-9*

1977

novel of the year
historical
Mollie Hardwick
Beauty's daughter: The story of Lady Hamilton's lost child
Methuen, 1976. ISBN 0-413-45310-3*

modern
Anne Worboys
Every man a king
Hodder & Stoughton, 1976. ISBN 0-340-20194-0
Ulverscroft Large Print Books, 1979.
ISBN 0-7089-0360-6*

Netta Muskett award
No Award

1978

novel of the year
historical
Madeleine Brent
Merlin's keep
Souvenir Press, 1984. ISBN 0-285-62677-9*
Ulverscroft Large Print Books, 1979.
ISBN 0-7089-0283-9*

modern
Catherine Macarthur
It was the lark
Macdonald & Jane's, 1977. ISBN 0-354-04116-9
Ulverscroft Large Print Books, 1979.
ISBN 0-7089-0370-3*

Netta Muskett award
No Award

Romantic Novelists Association Awards

1979
novel of the year
historical

Josephine Edgar
Countess
Macdonald & Jane's, 1978. ISBN 0-354-04305-6
Magna Print Books, 1978. (large print ed.).
ISBN 0-86009-382-4*

modern

No Award

Netta Muskett
award

Margery Goulden
Mirage
Hale, 1980. ISBN 0-7091-7805-0

1980
novel of the year
historical

Joanna Trollope
Parson Harding's daughter
Hutchinson, 1979. ISBN 0-09-138330-7
Magna Print Books, 1982. (large print ed.).
ISBN 0-86009-382-4*

modern

Mary Howard
Mr Rodriguez
Collins, 1979. ISBN 0-00-221681-7
Ulverscroft Large Print Books, 1980.
ISBN 0-7089-0551-X*

Netta Muskett
award

Nina Tinsley
Quentin's island
Hale, 1981. ISBN 0-7091-8637-1
Ulverscroft Large Print Books, 1987.
ISBN 0-7089-6387-0*

1981
novel of the year
historical

Gwendoline Butler
The red staircase
Collins, 1980. ISBN 0-00-221621-3*

Netta Muskett
award

Samantha Harvey
The driftwood beach
Mills & Boon, 1981. ISBN 0-263-09885-0
Chivers Press, 1986. (large print ed.).
ISBN 0-7451-9145-2*

148

1982
novel of the year   **Valerie Fitzgerald**
Zemindar
Bodley Head, 1981. ISBN 0-370-30429-2*

Netta Muskett   **Annabel Murray**
award   *The Master of Camariguo*
Mills & Boon, 1982. ISBN 0-263-10088-X

1983
novel of the year   **Eva Ibbotson**
Magic flutes
Century, 1982. ISBN 0-7089-1557-4*

Netta Muskett   No Award
award

1984
novel of the year   **Sheila Walsh**
A highly respectable marriage
Hutchinson, 1983. ISBN 0-09-151050-3
Magna Print Books, 1986. (large print ed.).
ISBN 0-86009-768-4*

Netta Muskett   No Award
award

1985
novel of the year   **Rosie Thomas**
Sunrise
Piatkus, 1984. ISBN 0-86188-458-2*
Fontana, 1984. (pbk). ISBN 0-00-616900-7*

Netta Muskett   No Award
award

1986
novel of the year   **Brenda Jagger**
A song twice over
Collins, 1985. ISBN 0-00-2272720-7*
Fontana, 1986. (pbk). ISBN 0-00-617294-6*

Netta Muskett   **Linda Acaster**
award   *Hostage of the heart*
Mills & Boon, 1986. ISBN 0-263-10088-X

Romantic Novelists Association Awards

1987
novel of the year   **Marie Joseph**
A better world than this
Century, 1986. ISBN 0-7126-9528-1*
Ulverscroft Large Print Books.
ISBN 0-7089-8430-4*
Arrow, 1987. (pbk). ISBN 0-09-952430-9*

Netta Muskett   **Nina Lambert**
award
A place in the sun
Piatkus, 1986. ISBN 0-86188-570-8*
Chivers Press, 1988. (large print ed.).
ISBN 0-7451-0648-X*

1988
novel of the year   **Audrey Howard**
The juniper bush
Century, 1987. ISBN 0-7126-1139-8
Fontana, 1988. (pbk). ISBN 0-00-617546-5*

Netta Muskett   **Kathryn Blake**
award
The house on the hill
Hale, 1988. ISBN 0-7090-3302-8

41 Royal Society of Literature Award under the W. H. Heinemann Bequest

One, two or three prizes may be awarded annually. The purpose of the bequest is to encourage genuine contributions to literature. Preference is given to those publications which are less likely to command large scales – e.g. poetry, biography, criticism, philosophy, history – though novels, if of sufficient distinction, will not be overlooked. Preference is also given to the works of younger, less recognized authors.

Contact   Royal Society of Literature
1 Hyde Park Gardens
London W2 2LT
Tel. 01-723 5104

1975

Malcolm Bradbury
The history man
Secker & Warburg, 1975. ISBN 0-436-06502-9*
Arrow, 1977. (pbk). ISBN 0-09-914910-9*

William Trevor
Angels at the Ritz: And other stories
Bodley Head, 1975. ISBN 0-370-10603-2*

1976

Philip Ziegler
Melbourne: A biography of William Lamb, 2nd Viscount Melbourne
Collins, 1976. ISBN 0-00-216510-4
2nd ed. Collins, 1987. (pbk).
ISBN 0-00-217957-1*

Edward Cruikshank
The shadow of the Winter Palace: The drift to revolution, 1825–1917
Macmillan, 1977. ISBN 0-333-14882-7*
Papermac, 1986. (pbk). ISBN 0-333-39892-0*

1977

Christopher Hill
Milton and the English revolution
Faber & Faber, 1977. ISBN 0-571-10198-4*

F. S. L. Lyons
Charles Stuart Parnell
Collins, 1977. ISBN 0-00-211682-0

Norman and Jeanne Mackenzie
The first Fabians
Weidenfeld & Nicolson, 1977.
ISBN 0-297-77090-X

1978

Frank Tuohy
Live bait: And other stories
Macmillan, 1978. ISBN 0-333-23861-3

1979

Brian Fothergill
Beckford of Fonthill
Faber & Faber, 1979. ISBN 0-571-10794-X

Ted Hughes
Moortown
Faber & Faber, 1979. ISBN 0-571-11453-9*

1980

Robert Bernard Martin
Tennyson: The unquiet heart
Oxford University Press, 1980.
ISBN 0-19-812072-9*
Faber & Faber, 1983. (pbk).
ISBN 0-571-11842-9*

Dick Davis
Seeing the world
Anvil Press Poetry, 1980. (pbk).
ISBN 0-85646-061-3

RSL Award – Heinemann Bequest

1981

James Leigh Milne
Harold Nicolson: A biography
Chatto & Windus, 1980. ISBN 0-7011-2520-9
Vol. 1. Hamish Hamilton, 1987. (pbk).
ISBN 0-241-12354-2*
Vol. 2. Hamish Hamilton, 1988. (pbk).
ISBN 0-241-12182-5*

Jonathan Raban
Old glory
Collins, 1981. ISBN 0-00-216521-X*
Pan, 1986. (pbk). ISBN 0-330-29229-3*

1982

Derek Walcott
The fortunate traveller
Faber & Faber, 1982. (pbk).
ISBN 0-571-11893-3*

1983

Nicholas Gage
Eleni
Collins, 1983. ISBN 0-00-217147-3*
Fontana, 1984. (pbk). ISBN 0-00-636865-9*

1984

Peter Ackroyd
T. S. Eliot
Hamish Hamilton, 1984. ISBN 0-241-11349-0*

Hilary Spurling
Secrets of a woman's heart: The later life of Ivy Compton-Burnett: 1920–1969
Hodder & Stoughton, 1984. ISBN 0-340-26241-9
Penguin, 1986. (pbk). ISBN 0-14-058013-1*

1985

Brian Moore
Black robe
Cape, 1983. ISBN 0-224-02329-2
Grafton, 1987. (pbk). ISBN 0-586-08615-3*

RSL Award – Heinemann Bequest

1986

Richard Dawkins
The blind watchmaker
Longman, 1986. ISBN 0-582-44694-5*
Penguin, 1988. (pbk). ISBN 0-14-008056-2*

1987

Michael Ignatieff
The Russian album
Chatto & Windus, 1987. ISBN 0-7011-3109-8*
Penguin, 1988. (pbk). ISBN 0-14-0088-8-3*

42 Runciman Award

The prize, of £1,000, is offered by the Anglo-Hellenic League and made possible by the generosity of the Onassis Foundation and is awarded to a book about Greece.

Contact	Book Trust Book House 45 East Hill London SW18 2QZ Tel. 01-870 9055

1986

    David Constantine
Early Greek travellers and the Hellenic ideal
Cambridge University Press, 1984.
ISBN 0-521-25342-X*

1987   No Award

1988

    John S. Koliopoulos
Brigands with a cause: Brigandage and irredentism in modern Greece, 1821–1912
Oxford University Press, 1987.
ISBN 0-19-822863-5*

1989

    Rowland J. Mainstone
Hagia Sophia
Thames & Hudson, 1989.
ISBN 0-500-34098-6*

43 The Saltire Society and *The Scotsman* Literary Awards

The award, of £1,500, sponsored by *The Scotsman*, is for the Scottish book of the year. In 1988 an award of £1,000 for the best first work was given.

Contact The Saltire Society
9 Fountain Close
High Street
Edinburgh EH1 1TF
Tel. (031) 556 1836

1982

Alasdair Gray
Lanark: A life in four books
Canongate, 1981. ISBN 0-903937-74-3*
Grafton, 1987. (pbk). ISBN 0-586-08613-7*

1983

Derick Thomson
Collected poems, 1940–1980
Macdonald, 1982. ISBN 0-904265-57-9*

Edwin Morgan
Poems of thirty years
Carcanet Press, 1982. ISBN 0-85635-365-5*

1984

David Daiches
God and the poets: The Gifford lectures
Clarendon Press, 1983. ISBN 0-19-812825-8

Tom Leonard
Intimate voices: Selected works, 1965–1983
Galloping Dog Press, 1984. ISBN 0-904837-68-8*

Saltire Society and The Scotsman Literary Awards

1985

Norman MacCaig
Collected poems
Chatto & Windus, 1985. ISBN 0-7011-3953-6
Chatto & Windus, new ed. 1988. (pbk).
ISBN 0-7011-3335-X*

1986

Stuart Hood
A storm from paradise
Carcanet Press, 1985. ISBN 0-85635-582-8*
Grafton, 1988. (pbk). ISBN 0-586-08716-8*

1987

Muriel Spark
The stories of Muriel Spark
Bodley Head, 1987. ISBN 0-370-31020-9*

1988
book of the year

Neal Acherson
Games with shadows
Century Hutchinson, 1988. ISBN 0-09-173019-8*

Tom Nairn
The enchanted glass: Britain and its monarchy
Century Hutchinson, 1988. ISBN 0-09-172960-2*
Century Hutchinson, 1988. (pbk).
ISBN 0-09-172955-6*

best first book
of the year

Raymond Vettese
The richt noise
Macdonald, 1988. ISBN 0-86334-062-8*

44 Science Book Prize

Founded in 1988 to encourage the public understanding of science and technology, the prize, of £1,000, is for a popular non-fiction book.

Contact Committee on the Public Understanding of
Science
6 Carlton House Terrace
London SW1Y 5AG
Tel. 01-839 5561

1988

British Medical Association Board of Science
Living with risk
BMA/John Wiley, 1987. ISBN 0-471-91598-X*

1989

Roger Lewin
Bones of contention
Simon & Schuster, 1989. ISBN 0-671-52688-X*

45 Scottish Arts Council Book Awards

Awards of £750 in the spring and autumn of each year for new writing by Scottish authors.

Contact Literature Department
Scottish Arts Council
19 Charlotte Square
Edinburgh EH2 4DF
Tel. (031) 226 6501

Spring 1981

David Kerr Cameron
Willie Gavin, crofter man: Portrait of a vanished lifestyle
Gollancz, 1980. ISBN 0-575-02816-5

Robert A. Crampsey
The Edinburgh pirate
Canongate, 1980. ISBN 0-903937-65-4

Bernard Maclaverty
Lamb
Cape, 1980. ISBN 0-224-01815-9*
Penguin, 1988. (pbk). ISBN 0-14-010811-4*

Tessa Ransford
Light of mind: dulce lumen, triste lumen, suave lumen, flecke: Selected poems
Ramsey Head Press, 1980. ISBN 0-902859-73-0

Frances J. Shaw
The Northern and Western Islands of Scotland
John Donald, 1980. ISBN 0-85976-059-6*

Autumn 1981

Anne Smith
Magic glass
Michael Joseph, 1981. ISBN 0-7181-1986-X

Scottish Arts Council Book Awards

Alasdair Gray
Lanark: A life in four books
Canongate, 1981. ISBN 0-903937-74-3*
Grafton, 1987. (pbk). ISBN 0-586-08613-7*

Olive Checkland
Philanthropy in Victorian Scotland: Social welfare and the voluntary principle
John Donald, 1980. ISBN 0-85976-041-3

Geoffrey W. S. Barrow
Kingship and unity: Scotland 1000–1306
Edward Arnold, 1981. ISBN 0-7131-6306-2

Jeremy Wormald
Court, Kirk and community
Edward Arnold, 1981. ISBN 0-7131-6310-0*
Edward Arnold, 1981. (pbk).
ISBN 0-7131-6311-9*

Spring 1982

Angus Calder
Revolutionary empire: Rise of the English speaking empire from the fifteenth century to the 1780s
Cape, 1981. ISBN 0-224-01452-8*

Francis Russell Hart and J. B. Pick
Neil M. Gunn: A highland life
John Murray, 1981. ISBN 0-7195-3856-4*

Christina Larner
Enemies of God: Witch hunt in Scotland
Chatto & Windus, 1981. ISBN 0-7011-2424-5
New ed. Blackwell, 1983. (pbk).
ISBN 0-631-13493-X*

Michael Lynch
Edinburgh and the Reformation
John Donald, 1981. ISBN 0-85976-069-3*

Alan Massie
Death of men
Bodley Head, 1981. ISBN 0-370-30339-3
Robin Clark, 1982. (pbk). ISBN 0-86072-060-8*

Scottish Arts Council Book Awards

Christine Miller
A childhood in Scotland
John Murray, 1981. ISBN 0-7195-3830-0

Ken Morrice
For all I know
Aberdeen University Press, 1981.
ISBN 0-08-025756-9*

Autumn 1982

Geoffrey Finlayson
The Seventh Earl of Shaftesbury
Methuen, 1981. ISBN 0-413-28200-7*

Bernard MacLaverty
A time to dance: And other stories
Cape, 1982. ISBN 0-224-02018-8*
Penguin, 1985. (pbk). ISBN 0-14-006852

Tom McNab
Flannagan's run
Hodder & Stoughton, 1980.
ISBN 0-340-24393-7*
Ulverscroft Large Print Books, 1983.
ISBN 0-7089-8142-9*

Eric Richards
A history of the Highland clearances: Agrarian transformations and the evictions, 1746–1886
Vol. 1. Croom Helm, 1982. ISBN 0-85664-496-X
Vol. 2. Croom Helm, 1985. ISBN 0-7099-2259-0*

Iain Crichton Smith
Selected poems: 1955–1980
Macdonald, 1982. ISBN 0-904265-55-2*
Macdonald, 1982. (pbk). ISBN 0-904265-56-0*

Spring 1983

Ron Butlin
The exquisite instrument
Salamander Press, 1982. ISBN 0-907540-13-9
Salamander Press, 1982. (pbk).
ISBN 0-907540-14-7*

Scottish Arts Council Book Awards

Ian Cowan
The Scottish Reformation: Church and society in sixteenth century Scotland
Weidenfeld & Nicolson, 1982.
ISBN 0-297-78029-8*

Eileen Dunlop
The maze stone
Oxford University Press, 1982.
ISBN 0-19-271458-9*

Kathleen Jamie
Black spiders
Salamander Press, 1982. ISBN 0-907540-15-5
Salamander Press, 1982. (pbk).
ISBN 0-907540-16-3*

Trevor Royle
Death before dishonour: The true story of fighting Mac: Major-General Sir Hector MacDonald
Mainstream Publishing, 1982.
ISBN 0-906391-30-X

William Watson
The knight on the bridge
Chatto & Windus, 1982. ISBN 0-7011-2635-3

Autumn 1983

Tom Gallacher
Apprentice
Hamish Hamilton, 1983. ISBN 0-241-10997-3*
Sceptre, 1988. (pbk). ISBN 0-340-42145-2*

Alasdair Gray
Unlikely stories mostly
Canongate, 1983. ISBN 0-86241-029-0
Penguin, 1984. (pbk). ISBN 0-14-006925-9*

James Kelman
Not, not while the giro: And other stories
Polygon, 1983. ISBN 0-904919-61-7
Polygon, 1983. (pbk). ISBN 0-904919-65-X*

Scottish Arts Council Book Awards

Lyn Macdonald
Somme
Michael Joseph, 1983. ISBN 0-7181-2254-2*
Papermac, 1984. (pbk). ISBN 0-333-36648-4*

Bernard MacLaverty
Cal
Cape, 1983. ISBN 0-224-02062-5*
Heinemann Educational, 1988.
ISBN 0-435-12336-X*
Penguin, 1988. (pbk). ISBN 0-14-010810-6*

Christopher Rush
Peace comes dropping slow
Ramsey Head Press, 1983. ISBN 0-902859-78-1*

Spring 1984

R. D. Anderson
Education and opportunity in Victorian Scotland: Schools and universities
Oxford University Press, 1983.
ISBN 0-19-822696-9*

Ron Butlin
The tilting room
Canongate, 1983. ISBN 0-86241-050-9*
Canongate, 1983. (pbk). ISBN 0-86241-051-7*

Gordon Donaldson
All the Queen's men: Power and politics in Mary Stewart's Scotland
Batsford, 1983. ISBN 0-7134-2347-1*

Harry Horse
The Ogopogo, or, my journey with the Loch Ness monster
Macdonald, 1983. ISBN 0-86334-016-4*

Norman MacCaig
A world of difference
New ed. Chatto & Windus, 1988.
ISBN 0-7011-3335-X*

Scottish Arts Council Book Awards

Ruth Ratcliff
Heritage and the Kaiser's children: An autobiography
Canongate, 1983. ISBN 0-86241-046-0

Autumn 1984

Frank Kuppner
A bad day for the Sung dynasty
Carcanet Press, 1984. (pbk).
ISBN 0-85635-514-3*

Liz Lochhead
Dreaming of Frankenstein: And collected poems
Polygon, 1984. (pbk). ISBN 0-904919-80-3*

Brian McCabe
Spring's witch
Mariscat Press, 1984. (pbk).
ISBN 0-946588-03-1*

Alasdair Maclean
Night falls on Ardnamurchan: The twilight of a crofting family
Gollancz, 1984. ISBN 0-575-03460-2
Penguin, 1988. (pbk). ISBN 0-14-007968-8*

George Mackay Brown
Time in a red coat
Chatto & Windus, 1984. ISBN 0-7011-2804-6

Agnes Owens
Gentlemen of the West
Polygon, 1984. ISBN 0-904919-79-X

Spring 1985

John Barrington
Red sky at night: Autobiography
Michael Joseph, 1985. ISBN 0-7181-1808-1
Ulverscroft Large Print Books, 1986.
ISBN 0-7089-1412-8*
Pan, 1986. (pbk). ISBN 0-330-29090-8*

Scottish Arts Council Book Awards

John Kerr Cameron
Cornkister days: A portrait of a land and its rituals
Gollancz, 1984. ISBN 0-575-03492-0*
Penguin, 1987. (pbk). ISBN 0-14-010097-0*

Ronald Frame
A winter journey
Bodley Head, 1984. ISBN 0-370-30663-5*
Grafton, 1986. (pbk). ISBN 0-586-06644-6*

Eugenie Fraser
The house by the Dvina: A Russian childhood
Mainstream Publishing, 1984.
ISBN 0-906391-69-5
Corgi, 1986. (pbk). ISBN 0-552-12833-3*

Valerie Gillies
Bed of stone
Canongate, 1984. ISBN 0-86241-060-6*

Edwin Morgan
Sonnets from Scotland
Mariscat Press, 1984. ISBN 0-946588-05-8*
Mariscat Press, 1984. (pbk).
ISBN 0-946588-06-6*

Alfred Smyth
Warlords and Holy Men
Edward Arnold, 1984. (pbk).
ISBN 0-7131-6305-4*

Autumn 1985

Ron Butlin
Ragtime in unfamiliar bars
Secker & Warburg, 1985. (pbk).
ISBN 0-436-07810-4*

Douglas Dunn
Elegies
Faber & Faber, 1985. ISBN 0-571-13570-6*
Faber & Faber, 1985. (pbk).
ISBN 0-571-13469-6*

Scottish Arts Council Book Awards

Elspeth Davie
A traveller's room
Hamish Hamilton, 1985. ISBN 0-241-11439-X*

Brian McCabe
Lipstick circus: And other stories
Mainstream Publishing, 1985.
ISBN 0-906391-87-3*
Mainstream Publishing, 1985. (pbk).
ISBN 0-906391-88-1*

William Neill
Wild places: Poems in three Leids
Luath Press, 1985. ISBN 0-946487-11-1*

Christopher Rush
A twelvemonth and a day
Aberdeen University Press, 1985.
ISBN 0-08-032428-2*
Aberdeen University Press, 1986. (pbk).
ISBN 0-08-032469-X*

Spring 1986

Roger Bilcliffe
The Glasgow boys: Glasgow School of Painting, 1875–1895
John Murray, 1955. ISBN 0-7195-4118-2*

Carol Ann Duffy
Standing female nude
Anvil Poetry Press, 1985. (pbk).
ISBN 0-85646-150-4*

Paul Hyde
Details from an apocalypse: Short stories
Albyn Press, 1985. ISBN 0-284-98740-9*

Jessie Kesson
Where the apple ripens
Chatto & Windus, 1985. ISBN 0-7011-3974-9
Hogarth Press, 1986. (pbk). ISBN 0-7012-0738-8*

Scottish Arts Council Book Awards

Norman MacCaig
Collected poems
Chatto & Windus, 1985. ISBN 0-7011-3953-6
New ed. Chatto & Windus, 1988. (pbk).
ISBN 0-7011-3335-X*

Sorley Maclean
Ris a' Bruthaich: Criticism and prose writing
Acair, 1985. ISBN 0-86152-013-0*
Acair, 1985. (pbk). ISBN 0-86152-041-6*

Autumn 1986

Anne Fine
The killjoy
Transworld, 1987. (pbk). ISBN 0-552-99257-7*
Bantam, 1985. (pbk). ISBN 0-593-01015-9*

Colin Mackay
Song of the forest
Canongate, 1986. ISBN 0-86241-114-9*
Fontana, 1987. (pbk). ISBN 0-00-654211-5*

Eileen Dunlop
Clementina
Oxford University Press, 1985.
ISBN 0-19-271503-8*

Tom Gallacher
The jewel maker
Hamish Hamilton, 1986. ISBN 0-241-11866-2

James Hunter and Cailean Maclean
Skye: The island
Mainstream Publishing, 1986.
ISBN 1-85158-017-4*

Spring 1987

Iain Banks
The bridge
Macmillan, 1986. ISBN 0-333-41285-0*
Futura, 1986. (pbk). ISBN 0-7088-8303-6*

Scottish Arts Council Book Awards

Ronald Frame
A long weekend with Marcel Proust: Seven short stories and a novel
Bodley Head, 1986. ISBN 0-370-31015-2*
Sceptre, 1988. (pbk). ISBN 0-340-42891-0*

Frances Mary Hendry
Quest for a kelpie
Canongate, 1986. ISBN 0-86241-128-9*
Canongate, 1987. (pbk). ISBN 0-86241-136-X*

Alan Massie
Augustus
Bodley Head, 1986. ISBN 0-370-30757-7*
Sceptre, 1987. (pbk). ISBN 0-340-41224-0*

Margaret H. B. Sanderson
Cardinal of Scotland: David Beaton, 1494–1546
John Donald, 1986. ISBN 0-85976-110-X*

Autumn 1987

G. F. Dutton
Squaring the waves
Bloodaxe, 1986. (pbk). ISBN 1-85224-007-5*

James Kelman
Greyhound for breakfast
Sidgwick & Jackson, 1987. ISBN 0-436-23283-9*
Pan, 1988. (pbk). ISBN 0-330-30027-X*

Andro Linklater
Compton Mackenzie: A life
Chatto & Windus, 1987. ISBN 0-7011-2583-7*

Brian McCabe
One atom to another
Polygon, 1987. (pbk). ISBN 0-948275-22-7*

Alastair Mackie
Ingaitherins: Selected poems
Aberdeen University Press, 1987. (pbk).
ISBN 0-08-035071-2*

Scottish Arts Council Book Awards

Tom Pow
Rough seas
Canongate, 1987. (pbk). ISBN 0-86241-150-5*

Duncan and Linda Williamson
A thorn in the King's foot: Folktales of the Scottish travelling people
Penguin, 1987. (pbk). ISBN 0-14-059508-2*

Spring 1988

William Boyd
The new confessions
Hamish Hamilton, 1987. ISBN 0-241-12383-6*
Penguin, 1988. (pbk). ISBN 0-14-010699-5*

Annette Hope
A Caledonian feast: Scottish cuisine through the ages
Mainstream Publishing, 1987.
ISBN 0-85158-077-8*
Grafton, 1989. (pbk). ISBN 0-586-20304-4*

Ian Jack
Before the oil ran out: Britain, 1978–1986
Secker & Warburg, 1987. ISBN 0-436-22020-2*
Fontana, 1988. (pbk). ISBN 0-00-654313-8*

Kathleen Jamie
The way we live
Bloodaxe, 1987. (pbk). ISBN 1-85224-034-2*

Bernard MacLaverty
The Great Profundo: And other stories
Cape, 1987. ISBN 0-224-02483-3*

Elma Mitchell
People etcetera: Poems now and selected
Peterloo Poets, 1987. ISBN 0-905291-84-0*

Autumn 1988

John Burnside
The hoop
Carcanet Press, 1988. ISBN 0-85635-742-1*

Frederic Lindsay
A charm against drowning
Deutsch, 1988. ISBN 0-233-98254-X*

Norman MacCaig
Voice-over
Chatto & Windus, 1988. (pbk).
ISBN 0-7011-3313-9*

Candida McWilliam
A case of knives
Bloomsbury Publishing, 1987.
ISBN 0-7475-0074-6*

Edwin Morgan
Themes on a variation
Carcanet Press, 1988. ISBN 0-85635-778-2*

46 SCSE Book Prizes

The prizes, of £1,000 and £500, are awarded by the Standing Conference in Studies in Education for the best books on education published during the preceding year.

Contact   Standing Conference in Studies in Education
University of Durham
School of Education
Leazes Road
Durham DH1 1TA
Tel. (091) 374 3497 or (091) 386 8908

1982/3

David H. Hargreaves
The challenge for the comprehensive school: Culture, curriculum and community
Routledge & Kegan Paul, 1982. (pbk).
ISBN 0-7100-0981-X*

Linda Pollock
Forgotten children: Parent/child relationships from 1500–1800
Cambridge University Press, 1983.
ISBN 0-521-25009-9*
Cambridge University Press, 1983. (pbk).
ISBN 0-521-27133-9*

1984

G. H. Bantock
Studies in the history of educational theory. Vol. 2: The minds and the masses, 1760–1980
Allen & Unwin, 1984. ISBN 0-04-370119-1*

P. Gardner
The lost elementary schools of Victorian England: The people's education
Croom Helm, 1984. ISBN 0-7099-1156-4*

1985

N. Beattie
Professional parents: Parent participation in four Western European countries
Falmer Press, 1985. ISBN 1-85000-077-8*
Falmer Press, 1985. (pbk).
ISBN 1-85000-078-6*

joint 2nd

Brian J. Salter and T. Tapper
Power and policy in education: The case of independent schooling
Falmer Press, 1985. ISBN 1-85000-062-X*
Falmer Press, 1985. (pbk).
ISBN 1-85000-063-8*

P. Croll and D. Moses
Out in five: Assessment and incidence of special educational needs
Routledge & Kegan Paul, 1985.
ISBN 0-7102-0322-5*

1986

M. Hughes
Children and number
Blackwell, 1986. ISBN 0-631-13581-2*

Peter Slee
Learning and liberal education: The study of modern history in the Universities of Oxford, Cambridge and Manchester
Manchester University Press, 1986.
ISBN 0-7190-1896-X*
Manchester University Press, 1988. (pbk).
ISBN 0-7190-2365-3*

1987

Stephen Ball
The micro-politics of the school: Towards a theory of school organization
Methuen, 1987. ISBN 0-416-00102-5*
Methuen, 1987. (pbk). ISBN 0-416-00112-2*

A. Bell and A. Sigsworth
The small rural primary school
Falmer Press, 1982. ISBN 1-85000-155-3*

47 Silver Pen Awards

The Silver Pen Awards, with categories for fiction and non-fiction, have been presented since 1969. In 1986 the awards were divided into two: the Macmillan Silver Pen Award, of £500, is now given for an outstanding work of fiction, the Time Life Silver Pen Award, of £1,000, for works of non-fiction.

Contact   The Centre for International PEN
7 Dilke Street
London SW3 4JE
Tel. 01-352 6303

1969
fiction

John Fowles
The French Lieutenant's woman
Cape, 1969. ISBN 0-224-61654-4*
Pan, 1987. (pbk). ISBN 0-330-29811-9*

non-fiction

Sir Stephen Runciman
The Great Church in captivity: Study of the Patriarchate of Constantinople from the eve of the Turkish conquest to the Greek War of Independence
Cambridge University Press, 1968.
ISBN 0-521-07188-7
Cambridge University Press, 1985. (pbk).
ISBN 0-521-31310-4

1970
fiction

Melvyn Bragg
The hired man
Secker & Warburg, 1969. ISBN 0-436-06705-6*
Hodder & Stoughton, 1977. (pbk).
ISBN 0-340-21807-X*

non-fiction

Brian Fothergill
Sir William Hamilton: Envoy extraordinaire
Faber & Faber, 1969. ISBN 0-571-08958-5

Silver Pen Awards

1971
fiction   **Mary Renault**
Fire from heaven
Longman, 1970. ISBN 0-582-10134-4
Penguin, 1983. (pbk). ISBN 0-14-003222-3*

poetry   **Iain Crichton Smith**
Selected poems
Gollancz, 1970. ISBN 0-575-00545-9

science   **F. D. Ommaney**
Lost leviathan
Hutchinson, 1971. ISBN 0-09-105990-9

1973/4
fiction   **Storm Jameson**
There will be a short interval
Harvill Press, 1973. ISBN 0-00271809-X

                 Christopher Leach
The send off
Chatto & Windus, 1973. ISBN 0-7011-1966-7

biography   **V. S. Pritchett**
Balzac
Chatto & Windus, 1973. ISBN 0-7011-1932-2

(Awards were temporarily suspended 1975–1979)

1980
fiction   **Anne Chisholm**
Nancy Cunard
Sidgwick & Jackson, 1979. ISBN 0-283-98335-3
Penguin, 1981. (pbk). ISBN 0-14-005572-X*

1981
biography   **William Anderson**
Dante the maker
Routledge & Kegan Paul, 1980.
ISBN 0-7100-0322-6*
Hutchinson, 1983. (pbk). ISBN 0-09-153201-9*

Silver Pen Awards

1982
fiction

D. M. Thomas
The white hotel
Gollancz, 1981. ISBN 0-575-02889-0*
Penguin, 1982. (pbk). ISBN 0-14-006032-4*

1983
fiction

Christopher Hope
Private parts
Routledge & Kegan Paul, 1982.
ISBN 0-7100-0954-2*
Granada, 1983. (pbk). ISBN 0-586-05767-6*

1984
biography

Tony Gould
Insider outsider
Chatto & Windus, 1973. ISBN 0-7011-2678-7*
Penguin, 1986. (pbk). ISBN 0-14-008662-5*

1985
fiction

Colin Thubron
A cruel madness
Heinemann, 1984. ISBN 0-434-77987-3*
Penguin, 1985. (pbk). ISBN 0-14-007760-X*

1986
Macmillan Silver
Pen Award for
Fiction

A. S. Byatt
Still life
Chatto & Windus, 1985. ISBN 0-7011-2667-1*
Penguin, 1986. (pbk). ISBN 0-14-008703-6*

Time Life Silver
Pen Award for
Non-Fiction

Michael Scammell
Solzhenitsyn
Hutchinson, 1985. ISBN 0-09-151280-8*
Grafton, 1986. (pbk). ISBN 0-586-08538-6*

1987
Macmillan Silver
Pen Award for
Fiction

Lewis Nkosi
Mating birds
Constable, 1986. ISBN 0-09-467240-7*
Fontana, 1987. (pbk). ISBN 0-00-654187-9*

Silver Pen Awards

Time Life Silver Pen Award for Non-Fiction	**Patrick Leigh Fermor** *Between the woods and the water* John Murray, 1986. ISBN 0-7195-4264-2* Penguin, 1988. (pbk). ISBN 0-14-009430-X*

1988

Macmillan Silver Pen Award for Fiction	**A. L. Barker** *The gooseboy* Hutchinson, 1987. ISBN 0-09-172569-0*
Time Life Silver Pen Award for Non-Fiction	**John Miller** *Friends and Romans: On the run in wartime Italy* Fourth Estate, 1987. ISBN 0-947795-07-3*

1989

Macmillan Silver Pen Award for Fiction	**Molly Keane** *Loving and giving* Deutsch, 1989. ISBN 0-233-98346-5*
Time Life Silver Pen Award for Non-Fiction	**Brenda Maddox** *Nora: A biography of Nora Joyce* Hamish Hamilton, 1989. ISBN 0-241-12385-2*

48 André Simon Memorial Fund Book Awards

The awards, of £1,500 each, were inaugurated in memory of André Simon and are awarded for outstanding works on wine, drinks or beverages and food.

Contact   Secretary to the Fund
61 Church Street
Isleworth
Middlesex TW7 6BE
Tel. 01-560 6662

1981
food

Anne Willan
French regional cooking
Century, 1989. ISBN 0-7126-3026-0*

drink

John R. Hume and Michael S. Moss
The making of Scotch whisky: History of the Scotch whisky distilling industry
James & James, 1981. ISBN 0-907383-00-9

1982
food

Jane Grigson
Fruit book
Michael Joseph, 1982. ISBN 0-7181-2125-2*

Barbara Maher
Cakes
Norman & Hobhouse, 1982.
ISBN 0-906908-14-0*

drink

David Peppercorn
Bordeaux
Faber & Faber, 1982. ISBN 0-571-11758-9*

1983
food

Roger Phillips
Wild food
Peerage Books, 1988. ISBN 1-85052-105-0*
Pan, 1983. (pbk). ISBN 0-330-28069-4*

André Simon Memorial Fund Book Awards

drink **Hugh Johnson**
Wine companion
Mitchell Beazley, 1985. ISBN 0-85533-562-9*

1984
food **So Yan-Kit**
Yan-Kit's classic Chinese cookbook
Dorling Kindersley, 1984. ISBN 0-86318-025-6*
Dorling Kindersley, 1987. (pbk).
ISBN 0-86318-259-3*

drink **Rosemary George**
The wines of Chablis
Sotheby's Publications, 1984.
ISBN 0-85667-179-7*

1985
food **Hannah Wright**
Soups
J. Norman, 1985. ISBN 0-7090-2491-6*
J. Norman, 1985. (pbk). ISBN 0-7090-2054-6*

drink **Nicholas Belfrage**
Life beyond Lambrusco: Understanding Italian fruit wine
Sidgwick & Jackson, 1985.
ISBN 0-283-99271-9*
Sidgwick & Jackson, 1985. (pbk).
ISBN 0-283-99272-7*

1986
food **Harold McGee**
On food and cooking: The science and lore of the kitchen
Allen & Unwin, 1986. ISBN 0-04-306003-X*
Unwin Hyman, 1988. (pbk).
ISBN 0-04-440277-5*

drink **Jancis Robinson**
Vines, grapes and wines
Mitchell Beazley, 1986. ISBN 0-85533-581-5*

André Simon Memorial Fund Book Awards

1987
food **Henrietta Green**
British food finds: A directory of fine British foods
Rich & Green, 1987. ISBN 0-9511870-0-2

drink **Stephen Brook**
Liquid gold: Dessert wines of the world
Constable, 1987. ISBN 0-09-466920-1*

49 W. H. Smith Literary Award

The award, of £10,000, is made to a UK or Commonwealth author whose work has made the most outstanding contribution to literature.

Contact Public Relations
W. H. Smith
7 Holbein Place
London SW1W 8NR
Tel. 01-730 1200 ext. 5448

1959

Patrick White
Voss
Cape, 1980. ISBN 0-224-01773-X*
Penguin, 1970. (pbk). ISBN 0-14-001438-1*

1960

Laurie Lee
Cider with Rosie
Hogarth Press, 1959. ISBN 0-7012-0157-6*
Chivers Press, 1977. (large print ed.).
ISBN 0-85997-265-8*
Longman, 1979. (pbk). ISBN 0-582-53678-2*
Penguin, 1970. (pbk). ISBN 0-14-001682-1*

1961

Nadine Gordimer
Friday's footprint
Gollancz, 1960. BNB B60-02023

1962

J. R. Ackerley
We think the world of you
Bodley Head, 1960. BNB B60-15867

1963

Gabriel Fielding
The birthday king
Hutchinson, 1962. BNB 862-15952

W. H. Smith Literary Award

1964
    Ernest H. Gombrich
    Meditations on a hobby horse, or, the roots of artistic form
    Phaidon Press, 1963. BNB B64-02699
    4th ed. Phaidon Press, 1985. (pbk).
    ISBN 0-7148-2379-1*

1965
    Leonard Woolf
    Beginning again: Autobiography of the years, 1911-1918
    Hogarth Press, 1964. BNB B64-09502

1966
    R. C. Hutchinson
    A child possessed
    Geoffrey Blef, 1964. BNB B64-17030

1967
    Jean Rhys
    Wide Sargasso sea
    Deutsch, 1966. ISBN 0-233-95866-5*
    Penguin, 1987. ISBN 0-14-008912-8*

1968
    V. S. Naipaul
    The mimic men
    Deutsch, 1967. BNB B67-09250

1969
    Robert Gittings
    John Keats
    Heinemann, 1968. BNB B68-03766
    Penguin, 1985. (pbk). ISBN 0-14-058005-0*

1970
    John Fowles
    The French Lieutenant's woman
    Cape, 1969. ISBN 0-224-01034-4*
    Methuen, 1982. (pbk). ISBN 0-413-48680-X*
    Pan, 1987. (pbk). ISBN 0-330-29811-9*

W. H. Smith Literary Award

1971
Nan Fairbrother
New lives, new landscapes
Architectural Press, 1970. ISBN 0-85139-483-3

1972
Kathleen Raine
The lost country
Dolmen Press, 1971. ISBN 0-85105-194-4

1973
Brian Moore
Catholics
Cape, 1972. ISBN 0-224-00767-X*
Granada, 1983. (pbk). ISBN 0-586-05695-4*

1974
Anthony Powell
Temporary kings
Heinemann, 1973. ISBN 0-434-59920-4*
Fontana, 1983. (pbk). ISBN 0-00-654055-4*

1975
Jon Stallworthy
Wilfred Owen: A biography
Oxford University Press, 1974.
ISBN 0-19-211719-X
Oxford University Press, 1988. (pbk).
ISBN 0-19-282211-X*

1976
Seamus Heaney
North
Faber & Faber, 1975. ISBN 0-571-10564-5
Faber & Faber, 1975. (pbk).
ISBN 0-571-10813-X*

1977
Ronald Lewin
Slim, the standard bearer: Biography of Field Marshal the Viscount Slim
Cooper, 1976. ISBN 0-85052-218-8

W. H. Smith Literary Award

1978

    Patrick Leigh Fermor
A time of gifts
John Murray, 1977. ISBN 0-7195-3348-1*

1979

    Mark Girouard
Life in the English country house
Yale University Press, 1978.
ISBN 0-300-02273-5*
Penguin, 1980. (pbk). ISBN 0-14-005406-5*

1980

    Thom Gunn
Selected poems: 1950–1975
Faber & Faber, 1979. ISBN 0-571-11512-8*
Faber & Faber, 1979. (pbk).
ISBN 0-571-11465-2*

1981

    Isabel Colegate
The shooting party
Hamish Hamilton, 1980. ISBN 0-241-10473-4
Penguin, 1982. (pbk). ISBN 0-14-005797-8*

1982

    George Clare
Last waltz in Vienna: The destruction of a family, 1842–1942
Macmillan, 1981. ISBN 0-333-32212-6*
Ulverscroft Large Print Books, 1983.
ISBN 0-7089-1018-1*
Pan, 1982. (pbk). ISBN 0-330-26780-9*

1983

    A. N. Wilson
Wise virgin
Secker & Warburg, 1982. ISBN 0-14-006661-6*

1984

    Philip Larkin
Required writing: Miscellaneous pieces, 1955–1962
Faber & Faber, 1984. ISBN 0-571-13481-5*
Faber & Faber, 1983. (pbk).
ISBN 0-571-13120-4*

W. H. Smith Literary Award

1985

David Hughes
The pork butcher
Constable, 1984. ISBN 0-09-465510-3*
Penguin, 1985. (pbk). ISBN 0-14-007647-6*

1986

Doris Lessing
The good terrorist
Cape, 1985. ISBN 0-224-02323-3*
Grafton, 1986. (pbk). ISBN 0-586-06880-5*

1987

Elizabeth Jennings
Collected poems: 1953–1985
Carcanet Press, 1986. ISBN 0-85635-648-4*
Carcanet Press, 1987. (pbk).
ISBN 0-85635-721-9*

1988

Robert Hughes
The fatal shore: History of the transportation of convicts to Australia, 1787–1868
Collins Harvill, 1987. ISBN 0-00-217361-1*
Pan, 1988. (pbk). ISBN 0-330-29892-5*

50 Southern Arts Literature Prize

The prize, now standing at £1,000, was first awarded in 1977 for the best work by an author living in the Southern Arts Region. In 1983 the prize has been offered each year for a different category in a three-year cycle: literary non-fiction, fiction, and poetry.

Contact   Southern Arts
            19 Southgate Street
            Winchester
            Hampshire SO23 9EB
            Tel. (0962) 55099

1977

Barbara Pym
Quartet in Autumn
Macmillan, 1977. ISBN 0-333-22778-6*
Grafton, 1980. (pbk). ISBN 0-586-05033-7*

1978

Penelope Lively
Nothing missing but the samovar: And other stories
Heinemann, 1978. ISBN 0-434-42736-5

1979

Craig Raine
A Martian sends a postcard home
Oxford University Press, 1979. (pbk).
ISBN 0-19-211896-X*

1980

John Fuller
The illusionists
Secker & Warburg, 1980. (pbk).
ISBN 0-436-16810-3*

A. N. Wilson
The healing art
Secker & Warburg, 1980. ISBN 0-436-57603-1*
Penguin, 1982. (pbk). ISBN 0-14-006122-3*

Southern Arts Literature Prize

1981
    Janice Elliott
    Secret places
    Hodder & Stoughton, 1981. ISBN 0-340-26247-8

    James Fenton
    A German requiem: A poem
    Salamander Press, 1981. (pbk). BNB B81-10397

1982   No Award

1983
non-fiction
    Peter Levi
    The flutes of autumn
    Harvill Press, 1983. ISBN 0-00-216246-6*
    Arrow, 1985. (pbk). ISBN 0-09-937620-2*

1984
fiction
    David Cook
    Sunrising
    Secker & Warburg, 1984. ISBN 0-436-10674-4*

1985
poetry
    Geoffrey Grigson
    Montaigne's tower: And other poems
    Secker & Warburg, 1984. ISBN 0-436-18806-6

1986
non-fiction
    Robert Gittings and Jo Manton
    Dorothy Wordsworth
    Oxford University Press, 1985.
    ISBN 0-19-818519-7*
    Oxford University Press, 1988. (pbk).
    ISBN 0-19-282048-6*

1987
fiction
    Grace Ingoldby
    Across the water
    Michael Joseph, 1985. ISBN 0-7181-2514-2
    Pan, 1986. (pbk). ISBN 0-330-29119-X*

1988
poetry
    David Constantine
    Madder
    Bloodaxe, 1987. (pbk). ISBN 1-85224-039-3*

51 Winifred Mary Stanford Prize

The prize, of £1,000, is awarded biennially to the work of an author under 50 which has been inspired by the Christian faith.

Contact Hodder & Stoughton
47 Bedford Square
London WC1B 3DP
Tel. 01-636 9851

1978

Jack Burton
Transport of delight
SCM Press, 1976. (pbk). ISBN 0-334-01682-7*

1980

John Whale
One church, one Lord
SCM Press, 1979. (pbk). ISBN 0-334-01184-1

1982

Monica Furlong
Merton: A biography
Darton, Longman & Todd, 1985.
ISBN 0-232-51649-9*

1984

Richard Holloway
The killing
Darton, Longman & Todd, 1983.
ISBN 0-232-51593-X*

1986

Tom Davies
Stained glass hours
New English Library, 1985. ISBN 0-450-06053-5

1988

Robert van de Weyer
Wickwyn: A vision for the future
SPCK, 1986. (pbk). ISBN 0-281-04212-8*

52 *Sunday Express* Book of the Year

Now the richest award for fiction in the UK, at £20,000, it is for a stylish novel which will reach a wide audience.

Contact Literary Editor
Sunday Express
121 Fleet Street
London EC4P 4JT
Tel. 01-353 8000

1987

Brian Moore
The colour of blood
Cape, 1987. ISBN 0-224-02513-9*
Isis Large Print Books, 1988.
ISBN 1-85089-248-2*
Grafton, 1988. (pbk). ISBN 0-586-08737-0*

shortlist

William Boyd
The new confessions
Hamish Hamilton, 1987. ISBN 0-241-12383-6*
Penguin, 1988. (pbk). ISBN 0-14-010699-5*

Ronald Hardy
Wings of the wind
Collins, 1987. ISBN 0-00-223109-3*
Fontana, 1988. (pbk). ISBN 0-00-617385-3*

Noel Virtue
The redemption of Elsden Bird
Peter Owen, 1987. ISBN 0-7206-0678-0*
Arrow, 1988. (pbk). ISBN 0-09-957530-2*

Mary Wesley
Not that sort of girl
Macmillan, 1987. ISBN 0-333-44552-X*
Transworld, 1988. (pbk). ISBN 0-552-99304-2*

1988

David Lodge
Nice work
Secker & Warburg, 1988. ISBN 0-436-25667-3*
Penguin, 1989. (pbk). ISBN 0-14-011920-5*

shortlist

Justin Cartwright
Interior
Hamish Hamilton, 1988. ISBN 0-241-12563-4*

Graham Greene
The captain and the enemy
Reinhardt Books, 1988. ISBN 1-871061-05-9*

Hilary Mantel
Eight weeks on Ghazzah Street
Viking, 1988. ISBN 0-670-82117-9*

Richard Rayner
Los Angeles without a map
Secker & Warburg, 1988. ISBN 0-436-40550-4*

Keith Waterhouse
Our song
Hodder & Stoughton, 1988.
ISBN 0-340-42501-6*

53 Betty Trask Awards

Awarded annually to an author of a published or unpublished first traditional or romantic novel. £12,500 is awarded to the winner or divided between joint winners with up to five runners-up receiving £1,000 each.

Contact	The Society of Authors 84 Drayton Gardens London SW10 9SB Tel. 01-373 6642

Titles which have not yet been published are marked NYP.

1984

Ronald Frame
Winter journey
Bodley Head, 1984. ISBN 0-370-30663-5*
Grafton, 1986. (pbk). ISBN 0-586-06644-6*

Clare Nonhebel
Cold showers
Century, 1985. ISBN 0-7126-0830-3
Grafton, 1986. (pbk). ISBN 0-586-06680-2*

runners-up

James Buchan
A parish of rich women
Hamish Hamilton, 1984. ISBN 0-241-11310-5*
Futura, 1987. (pbk). ISBN 0-7088-3370-5*

Helen Harris
Playing fields in winter
Century, 1986. ISBN 0-7126-9408-0

Gareth Jones
The disinherited
Gollancz, 1981. ISBN 0-575-02770-3

Simon Rees
The Devil's looking glass
Methuen, 1985. ISBN 0-413-57720-1

Betty Trask Awards

1985

Susan Kay
Legacy
Bodley Head, 1985. ISBN 0-370-30874-3*
Corgi, 1988. (pbk). ISBN 0-552-12720-5*

runners-up

Gary Armitage
A season of peace
Alison, 1985. ISBN 0-436-01809-8

Elizabeth Ironside
A very private enterprise
Hodder & Stoughton, 1984.
ISBN 0-340-35269-8*
Fontana, 1986. (pbk). ISBN 0-00-617280-6*

Alice Mitchell
Instead of Eden
W. H. Allen, 1986. ISBN 0-491-03873-9*

George Schweiz
The earth abides for ever
NYP

Caroline Stickland
The standing hills
Gollancz, 1986. ISBN 0-575-03809-8
Futura, 1988. (pbk). ISBN 0-7088-3654-2*

1986

Tim Parkes
Tongues of flame
Heinemann, 1985. ISBN 0-434-57735-9*
Fontana, 1986. (pbk). ISBN 0-00-617333-0*

Patricia Ferguson
Family myths and legends
Deutsch, 1985. ISBN 0-233-97726-0*
Penguin, 1986. (pbk). ISBN 0-14-008376-6*

runners-up

Philippa Blake
Muzungu's wife
Bodley Head, 1988. ISBN 0-370-31192-2*

Betty Trask Awards

1987

Matthew Kneale
Keiko
NYP

Kate Saunders
The prodigal father
Cape, 1986. ISBN 0-224-02361-6*
Grafton, 1987. (pbk). ISBN 0-586-07247-0*

James Maw
Hard luck
Quartet, 1986. ISBN 0-7043-2533-0*
Grafton, 1988. (pbk). ISBN 0-586-07369-8*

Peter Benson
The levels
Constable, 1987. ISBN 0-09-467680-1*
Penguin, 1988. (pbk). ISBN 0-14-010635-9*

Helen Flint
Return journey
Heinemann, 1987. ISBN 0-434-26700-7*
Transworld, 1988. (pbk). ISBN 0-552-99319-0*

runners-up

Catherine Arnold
Last time
Hodder & Stoughton, 1986.
ISBN 0-340-38783-1*

H. S. Bhabra
Gestures
Michael Joseph, 1986. ISBN 0-7181-2673-4*
Penguin, 1987. (pbk). ISBN 0-14-009265-X*

Lucy Pinney
The pink stallion
Hodder & Stoughton, 1988.
ISBN 0-340-42367-6*

1988

Alex Martin
The general interrupter
Viking, 1989. ISBN 0-670-82687-1*

Candida McWilliam
A case of knives
Bloomsbury, 1987. ISBN 0-7475-0074-6*

runners-up

Georgina Andrewes
Behind the waterfall
Pandora Press, 1988. ISBN 0-86358-249-4*
Unwin, 1989. (pbk). ISBN 0-04-440353-4*

James Friel
Left of North
Macmillan, 1987. ISBN 0-333-43346-7*
Futura, 1988. (pbk). ISBN 0-7088-3667-4*

Glenn Patterson
Burning your own
Chatto & Windus, 1988. ISBN 0-7011-3291-4*

Susan Webster
Small tales of a town
Simon & Schuster, 1988. ISBN 0-671-65529-9*

1989

Nigel Watts
The life game
Hodder & Stoughton, 1989.
ISBN 0-340-48791-7*

runners-up

Paul Houghton
Harry's last wedding
NYP

Alasdair McKee
Uncle Henry's last stand
Chatto & Windus, 1989. ISBN 0-7011-3448-8*

William Riviere
Watercolour sky
NYP

54 TSB Peninsula Prize

Launched in 1987, when no fewer than 190 novels were submitted, the award, of £1,000 and publication by Devon Books, is for the best unpublished novel by an author who is living in, or has strong links with, the region covered by South West Arts.

Contact   Literature Officer
South West Arts
Bradninch Place
Gandy Street
Exeter EX4 3LS
Tel. (0392) 218188

1987

N. R. Phillips
The saffron eaters
Devon Books, 1987. ISBN 0-86114-820-7*

1988

Steve May
Keeping faith
Devon Books, 1988. ISBN 0-86114-842-8*

55 Welsh Arts Council Awards

Five prizes of £1,000 each may be awarded annually in the following categories: poetry, fiction, non-fiction, literary criticism and young writer. Works eligible are by those who are Welsh by birth or resident in Wales, or which are of intimate interest to Wales.

Contact
Literature Officer
Welsh Arts Council
Museum Place
Cardiff CF1 3NX
Tel. (0222) 394711

1969

Raymond Garlick
A sense of Europe: Collected poems, 1954–1968
Gomer Press, 1968. ISBN 0-85088-012-2*

Glyn Jones
The dragon has two tongues: Essays on Anglo-Irish writers
Dent, 1968. ISBN 0-460-03650-5*

1970

John Ormond
Requiem and celebration
Christopher Davies, 1969. ISBN 0-85339-019-3

Harri Webb
The green desert: Collected poems, 1950–1969
Gwasg Gomer, 1969. BNB B70-09546

Sally Roberts Jones
Turning away: Collected poems, 1952–1968
Gwasg Gomer, 1969. ISBN 0-85088-042-4

1971

Dannie Abse
Selected poems
Hutchinson, 1970. ISBN 0-09-101200-7

Welsh Arts Council Awards

Joseph P. Clancy
The Earliest Welsh poetry
Macmillan, 1970. ISBN 0-333-10959-7

John Stuart Williams
Dic Penderyn: And other poems
Gwasg Gomer, 1970. ISBN 0-85088-076-9

1972

Emyr Humphries
National winner
Macdonald, 1971. ISBN 0-356-03597-2

Roland Mathias
Absalom in the tree: And other poems
Gwasg Gomer, 1971. ISBN 0-85088-114-5

Richard Jones
The tower is everywhere
Macmillan, 1971. ISBN 0-333-12654-8

1973

Iowerth C. Peate
Tradition and folk life: A Welsh view
Faber & Faber, 1972. ISBN 0-571-09804-5

R. S. Thomas
H'm: poems
Macmillan, 1975. ISBN 0-333-13807-4

Raymond Garlick
A sense of time: Poems and anti-poems, 1969–1972
Gwsag Gomer, 1972. ISBN 0-85088-146-3

Alison Morgan
Pete
Chatto & Windus, 1972. ISBN 0-7011-5010-6

1974

Alun Richards
Dai country: Short stories
Michael Joseph, 1973. ISBN 0-7181-1133-3

Welsh Arts Council Awards

John Ormond
Definition of a waterfall
Oxford University Press, 1973. (pbk).
ISBN 0-19-211830-7

1975

Peter Tinniswood
Except you're a bird
Hodder & Stoughton, 1974. ISBN 0-340-18568-6

Jeremy Hooker
Soliloquies of a chalk giant
Enitharmon Press, 1974. ISBN 0-90111-67-8

Leslie Norris
Mountains, polecats and pheasants: And other elegies
Chatto & Windus, 1974. ISBN 0-7011-1595-5

Emyr Humphries
Flesh and blood
Hodder & Stoughton, 1978. ISBN 0-340-23082-7
Sphere, 1986. (pbk). ISBN 0-7221-4785-6*

1976

Bernice Rubens
I sent a letter to my love
W. H. Allen, 1975. ISBN 0-491-01863-0
Abacus, 1982. (pbk). ISBN 0-349-13017-5*

R. S. Thomas
Laboratories of the spirit
Macmillan, 1975. ISBN 0-333-18510-2

Ruth Bigood
Not without homage
Christopher Davies, 1975. ISBN 0-7145-0191-2

Kenneth Morgan
Kier Hardie: Radical and socialist
Weidenfeld & Nicolson, 1975.
ISBN 0-297-76886-7
Weidenfeld & Nicolson, 1984. (pbk).
ISBN 0-297-78440-4*

Welsh Arts Council Awards

1977

Raymond Garlick
Incense: Poems, 1972–1975
Gwasg Gomer, 1976. ISBN 0-85088-339-3

Gwyn A. Williams
Goya and the impossible revolution
Allen Lane, 1976. ISBN 0-7139-0906-4

1978

Stuart Evans
The caves of alienation
Hutchinson, 1977. ISBN 0-09-128590-9

Paul Ferris
Dylan Thomas
Hodder & Stoughton, 1977. ISBN 0-340-19564-9
Penguin, 1985. (pbk). ISBN 0-14-058021-2*

Alice Thomas Ellis
The sin eater
Duckworth, 1977. ISBN 0-7156-0940-8*
Penguin, 1986. (pbk). ISBN 0-14-009202-1*

1979

Gillian Clarke
The sundial
J. D. Lewis, 1978. ISBN 0-85088-540-X*

James Hanley
A kingdom
Deutsch, 1978. ISBN 0-233-96972-1

Emyr Humphries
The best of friends
Hodder & Stoughton, 1978. ISBN 0-340-22964-0
Sphere, 1987. (pbk). ISBN 0-7221-4202-1*

Tristan Jones
The incredible voyage: A personal odyssey
Bodley Head, 1978. ISBN 0-370-30108-0
Ulverscroft Large Print Books, 1981.
ISBN 0-7089-8002-3*
Granada, 1984. (pbk). ISBN 0-586-06058-8*

Welsh Arts Council Awards

Leslie Norris
Sliding
Dent, 1978. ISBN 0-460-12038-7*
Longman, 1981. (pbk). ISBN 0-582-22066-1*

Gwyn Alfred Williams
The Merthyr rising
University of Wales Press, 2nd ed. 1988.
ISBN 0-7083-1014-1*

1980

Dannie Abse
Pythagoras
Hutchinson, 1979. ISBN 0-09-139431-7

Philip Owens
Look Christ
J. D. Lewis, 1979. (pbk). ISBN 0-85088-601-5*

Roland Mathias
Snipe's castle
J. D. Lewis, 1979. (pbk). ISBN 0-85088-741-0*

Robert Minhinnick
Native ground
Triskele Books, 1980. ISBN 0-904652-04-1*

Raymond Williams
The fight for Manod
Chatto & Windus, 1979. ISBN 0-13-647719-4
Hogarth Press, 1988. (pbk). ISBN 0-7012-0809-0*

1981

Jean Earle
A trial of strength
Carcanet Press, 1980. ISBN 0-85635-298-5
Carcanet Press, 1980. (pbk). ISBN
0-85635-298-5*

David Smith and Gareth Williams
Fields of praise: The official history of the Welsh Rugby Union, 1881–1981
University of Wales Press, 1980.
ISBN 0-7083-0766-3

Welsh Arts Council Awards

Nigel Wells
Winter festivals
Bloodaxe, 1980. (pbk). ISBN 0-906427-19-3*

1982

R. Merfyn Jones
The North Wales quarrymen, 1874–1922
University of Wales Press, 1981.
ISBN 0-7083-0776-0
University of Wales Press, new ed. 1982. (pbk).
ISBN 0-7083-0829-5*

Kenneth Morgan
Rebirth of a nation: Wales 1880–1980
Clarendon Press, 1982. ISBN 0-19-821736-6

1983

Rachel Bromwich
Dafydd ap Gwilym: Poems
Gwasg Gomer, 1982. ISBN 0-85088-815-8

Alice Thomas Ellis
The 27th kingdom
Duckworth, 1982. ISBN 0-7156-1645-5*
Penguin, 1986. (pbk). ISBN 0-14-006704-3*

1984

Duncan Bush
Aquarium
Poetry of Wales Press, 1983. (pbk).
ISBN 0-907476-15-5*

Emyr Humphries
The Taliesin tradition: A quest for Welsh identity
Black Raven Press, 1983. ISBN 0-85159-002-0

Sian James
Dragons and roses
Duckworth, 1983. ISBN 0-7156-1713-3

Mike Jenkins
Empire of smoke
Poetry of Wales Press, 1983.
ISBN 0-907476-28-7

Welsh Arts Council Awards

Robert Minhinnick
Life sentence
Poetry of Wales Press, 1983. (pbk).
ISBN 0-907476-17-1

1985

David Hughes
The pork butcher
Constable, 1984. ISBN 0-09-465510-3*
Penguin, 1985. (pbk). ISBN 0-14-007647-6*

Christopher Meredith
This
Poetry of Wales Press, 1984. (pbk).
ISBN 0-907476-39-2*

J. P. Ward
The clearing
Poetry of Wales Press, 1984.
ISBN 0-907476-34-1*

Ivor Wilks
South Wales and the rising of 1839
Croom Helm, 1984. ISBN 0-7099-2772-X*

1986

Duncan Bush
Salt: Poems
Poetry of Wales Press, 1983.
ISBN 0-907476-15-5*

Mary Jones
Resistance
Black Staff Press, 1985. (pbk).
ISBN 0-85640-330-X*

Christopher Norris
Contest of faculties
Methuen, 1985. (pbk). ISBN 0-416-39930-4

Oliver Reynolds
Skevington's daughter
Faber & Faber, 1985. ISBN 0-571-13697-4*
Faber & Faber, 1985. (pbk).
ISBN 0-571-13546-3*

Welsh Arts Council Awards

Raymond Williams
Loyalties
Chatto & Windus, 1985. ISBN 0-7011-2843-7

1987

Dannie Abse
Ask the bloody horse
Hutchinson, 1986. (pbk). ISBN 0-09-163971-9*

Stephen Gregory
The cormorant
Heinemann, 1986. ISBN 0-434-30576-6*
Sceptre, 1987. (pbk). ISBN 0-340-41690-4*

Douglas Houston
With the offal eaters
Bloodaxe, 1986. (pbk). ISBN 0-906427-70-3*

Frances Thomas
Seeing things
Gollancz, 1986. ISBN 0-575-03757-1*
Dent, 1987. (pbk). ISBN 0-460-02485-X*

Peter Thomas
Strangers from a secret land
Gomer Press, 1986. ISBN 0-86383-278-4*

1988

Hilary Llewellyn-Williams
The tree calendar: Poems
Poetry of Wales Press, 1987. (pbk).
ISBN 0-907476-77-5*

Sheenagh Pugh
Beware falling tortoises
Poetry of Wales Press, 1987. (pbk).
ISBN 0-907476-70-8*

Oliver Reynolds
The Player Queen's wife
Faber & Faber, 1987. ISBN 0-571-14998-7*
Faber & Faber, 1987. (pbk).
ISBN 0-571-14999-5*

Welsh Arts Council Awards

Bernice Rubens
Our father
Hamish Hamilton, 1984. ISBN 0-241-11979-0
Abacus, 1988. (pbk). ISBN 0-349-12904-5*

Glanmor Williams
Recovery, reorientation and reformation
Clarendon Press, 1988. ISBN 0-19-821733-1*

56 Whitbread Literary Awards

Five awards, of £1,500, can be given each year in the categories of: novel, first novel, biography, children's novel and poetry for works written by authors resident in the UK or the Republic of Ireland. From 1985 the judges have voted one book to be the Whitbread Book of the Year with a prize of £22,000.

Contact   The Booksellers Association of Great Britain and Ireland
154 Buckingham Palace Road
London SW1W 9TZ
Tel. 01-730 8214

The winners of the Children's Novel Award are listed below as they are eligible for the Book of the Year Award.

1971
novel

Gerda Charles
The destiny waltz
Eyre & Spottiswoode, 1971.
ISBN 0-413-44680-8*

biography

Michael Meyer
Henrik Ibsen: The farewell to poetry, 1864–1882
Hart-Davis, 1971. ISBN 0-246-64001-4

poetry

Geoffrey Hill
Mercian hymns
Deutsch, 1971. ISBN 0-223-95770-2
Deutsch, 1971. (pbk). ISBN 0-233-96794-X*

1972
novel

Susan Hill
Bird of night
Hamish Hamilton, 1972. ISBN 0-241-00258-4
Penguin, 1976. (pbk). ISBN 0-14-004072-2*

biography

James Pope-Hennessey
Trollope
Cape, 1971. ISBN 0-224-00611-8
Penguin, 1986. (pbk). ISBN 0-14-004072-2*

Whitbread Literary Awards

children's novel   **Rumer Godden**
The Diddakoi
Macmillan, 1972. ISBN 0-333-13848-1*
Penguin, 1975. (pbk). ISBN 0-14-030753-2*

1973
novel   **Shiva Naipaul**
The chip chip gatherers
Hamish Hamilton, 1983. ISBN 0-241-11020-3*
Longman, 1982. (pbk). ISBN 0-582-78553-7*

first novel   **Claire Tomalin**
The life and death of Mary Wollstonecraft
Weidenfeld & Nicolson, 1974.
ISBN 0-297-76754-2
Penguin, 1985. (pbk). ISBN 0-14-007266-7*

biography   **John Wilson**
C. B.: A life of Sir Henry Campbell-Bannerman
Constable, 1973. ISBN 0-09-458950-X*

children's novel   **Alan Aldridge and William Plomer**
The Butterfly Ball and the Grasshopper Feast
Cape, 1973. ISBN 0-224-00808-0

1974
novel   **Iris Murdoch**
The sacred and profane love machine
Chatto & Windus, 1987. ISBN 0-7011-3261-2*
Penguin, 1976. (pbk). ISBN 0-14-004111-7*

biography   **Andrew Boyle**
Poor dear Brendan: The quest for Brendan Bracken
Hutchinson, 1974. ISBN 0-09-120860-2

children's novel   **Russell Hoban and Quentin Blake**
How Tom beat Captain Najork and his hired sportsmen
Cape, 1974. ISBN 0-224-00999-0*

Jill Paton-Walsh
The Emperor's winding sheet
Macmillan, 1974. ISBN 0-333-15533-5*

Whitbread Literary Awards

1975
novel
    William McIlvanney
    Docherty
    Mainstream Publishing, 1983.
    ISBN 0-906391-36-9*
    Magna Print Books, 1986. (large print ed.).
    ISBN 0-86009-811-7*
    Sceptre, 1987. (pbk). ISBN 0-340-40757-3*

first book
    Ruth Spalding
    The improbable Puritan: A life of Bulstrade Whitelock
    Faber & Faber, 1975. ISBN 0-571-10626-9

autobiography
    Helen Corke
    In our infancy: An autobiography
    Cambridge University Press, 1975.
    ISBN 0-521-20797-5

1976
novel
    William Trevor
    The children of Dynmouth
    Bodley Head, 1976. ISBN 0-370-10561-3*
    Penguin, 1982. (pbk). ISBN 0-14-006263-7*

biography
    Winifred Gerin
    Elizabeth Gaskell: A biography
    Clarendon Press, 1976. ISBN 0-19-812070-2
    Oxford University Press, 1980. (pbk).
    ISBN 0-19-281296-3*

children's novel
    Penelope Lively
    A stitch in time
    Heinemann, 1976. ISBN 0-434-94897-7*
    Chivers Press, 1988. (large print ed.).
    ISBN 0-7451-0726-5*
    Penguin, 1986. (pbk). ISBN 0-14-031975-1*

1977
novel
    Beryl Bainbridge
    Injury time
    Duckworth, 1977. ISBN 0-7156-1246-8*
    Fontana, 1984. (pbk). ISBN 0-00-654004-X*

Whitbread Literary Awards

biography   **Nigel Nicolson**
Mary Curzon
Weidenfeld & Nicolson, 1977.
ISBN 0-297-77390-9

children's novel   **Shelagh Macdonald**
No end to yesterday
Deutsch, 1977. ISBN 0-233-96865-2*

1978
novel   **Paul Theroux**
Picture palace
Hamish Hamilton, 1978. ISBN 0-241-89991-5*
Penguin, 1979. (pbk). ISBN 0-14-005072-8*

biography   **John Grigg**
Lloyd George: The people's champion
Methuen, 1978. ISBN 0-413-32620-9*

children's novel   **Philippa Pearce**
The Battle of Bubble and Squeak
Deutsch, 1978. ISBN 0-233-96986-1*
Chivers Press, 1985. (large print ed.).
ISBN 0-7451-0134-8*
Macmillan Educational, 1983. (pbk).
ISBN 0-333-34190-2*
Penguin, 1980. (pbk). ISBN 0-14-031183-1*

1979
novel   **Jennifer Johnston**
The old jest
Hamish Hamilton, 1979. ISBN 0-241-10267-7*
G. K. Hall, 1981. (large print ed.).
ISBN 0-8161-3091-4*
Fontana, 1984. (pbk). ISBN 0-00-654051-1*

biography   **Penelope Mortimer**
About time: An aspect of autobiography
Allen Lane, 1979. ISBN 0-7278-0031-0

children's novel   **Peter Dickinson**
Tulku
Gollancz, 1979. ISBN 0-575-02503-4*

Whitbread Literary Awards

1980

novel — **David Lodge**
How far can you go?
Secker & Warburg, 1980. ISBN 0-436-25661-4*
Penguin, 1981. (pbk). ISBN 0-14-005746-3*

biography — **David Newsome**
On the edge of Paradise: A. C. Benson the diarist
John Murray, 1980. ISBN 0-7195-3690-1*

children's novel — **Leon Garfield**
John Diamond
Kestrel, 1980. ISBN 0-7226-5619-X*
Chivers Press, 1988. (large print ed.).
ISBN 0-7451-0757-5*
Penguin, 1981. (pbk). ISBN 0-14-031366-4*

1981

novel — **Maurice Leitch**
Silver's City
Secker & Warburg, 1981. ISBN 0-436-24413-6

first novel — **William Boyd**
A good man in Africa
Hamish Hamilton, 1981. ISBN 0-241-10516-1*
Magna Print Books, 1984. (large print ed.).
ISBN 0-86009-584-3*
Penguin, 1982. (pbk). ISBN 0-14-005887-7*

biography — **Nigel Hamilton**
Monty: The making of a General, 1887–1942
Hamish Hamilton, 1981. ISBN 0-241-10583-8*

children's novel — **Jane Gardam**
The hollow land
Heinemann Educational, 1983.
ISBN 0-435-12276-2*
Chivers Press, 1987. (large print ed.).
ISBN 0-7451-0495-9*
Penguin, 1983. (pbk). ISBN 0-14-031552-7*

1982

novel
John Wain
Young shoulders
Macmillan, 1982. ISBN 0-333-34055-8*
Macmillan Educational, 1988. (pbk).
ISBN 0-333-45659-9*

first novel
Bruce Chatwin
On the Black Hill
Cape, 1982. ISBN 0-224-01980-5*
Pan, 1983. (pbk). ISBN 0-330-28124-0*

biography
Edward Crankshaw
Bismarck
Macmillan, 1981. ISBN 0-333-34055-8
Papermac, 1982. (pbk). ISBN 0-333-34038-8*

children's novel
W. J. Corbett
The song of Pentecost
Methuen, 1982. ISBN 0-416-24730-X*
Chivers Press, 1988. (large print ed.).
ISBN 0-7451-0794-X*
Penguin, 1984. (pbk). ISBN 0-14-031689-2*

1983

novel
William Trevor
Fools of fortune
Bodley Head, 1983. ISBN 0-370-30953-7*

first novel
John Fuller
Flying to nowhere
Salamander Press, 1983. ISBN 0-907540-27-9*
Penguin, 1985. (pbk). ISBN 0-14-008055-4*

biography
Victoria Glendinning
Vita: The life of V. Sackville-West
Weidenfeld & Nicolson, 1983.
ISBN 0-297-78306-8*
Penguin, 1984. (pbk). ISBN 0-14-007161-X*

Kenneth Rose
King George V
Weidenfeld & Nicolson, 1983.
ISBN 0-297-78245-2
Papermac, 1984. (pbk). ISBN 0-333-37224-7*

Whitbread Literary Awards

children's novel
Roald Dahl
The witches
Cape, 1983. ISBN 0-224-02165-6*
Heinemann Educational, 1985.
ISBN 0-435-12293-2*
Penguin, 1985. (pbk). ISBN 0-14-031730-9*

1984
novel
Christopher Hope
Kruger's Alp
Heinemann, 1984. ISBN 0-434-34660-8*
Sphere, 1985. (pbk). ISBN 0-349-11715-2*

first novel
James Buchan
A parish of rich women
Hamish Hamilton, 1984. ISBN 0-241-11310-5*
Futura, 1987. (pbk). ISBN 0-7088-3370-5*

biography
Peter Ackroyd
T. S. Eliot
Hamish Hamilton, 1984. ISBN 0-241-11349-0*

children's novel
Barbara Willard
The Queen of the Pharisees' children
Julia Macrae, 1983. ISBN 0-86203-148-6*

1985
poetry and book of the year
Douglas Dunn
Elegies
Faber & Faber, 1985. ISBN 0-571-13570-6*
Faber & Faber, 1985. (pbk).
ISBN 0-571-13469-6*

novel
Peter Ackroyd
Hawksmoor
Hamish Hamilton, 1985. ISBN 0-241-11164-3*
Sphere, 1986. (pbk). ISBN 0-349-10057-8*

first novel
Jeanette Winterson
Oranges are not the only fruit
Pandora Press, 1985. (pbk). ISBN 0-86358-042-4*

biography
Ben Pimlott
Hugh Dalton
Cape, 1985. ISBN 0-224-02100-1*

Whitbread Literary Awards

children's novel   **Janni Howker**
The nature of the beast
Julia Macrae, 1985. ISBN 0-86203-194-X*
Armada, 1986. (pbk). ISBN 0-00-672582-1*
Macmillan, 1987. (pbk). ISBN 0-333-41374-X*

1986
novel and book of the year   **Kazuo Ishiguro**
An artist of the floating world
Faber & Faber, 1986. ISBN 0-571-13608-7*
Faber & Faber, 1987. (pbk).
ISBN 0-571-14716-X*

first novel   **Jim Crace**
Continent
Heinemann, 1986. ISBN 0-434-14824-5*
Pan, 1987. (pbk). ISBN 0-330-29964-6*

biography   **Richard Mabey**
Gilbert White
Century, 1986. ISBN 0-7126-1232-7*
Century, 1987. (pbk). ISBN 0-7126-1794-9*

poetry   **Peter Reading**
Stet
Secker & Warburg, 1986. ISBN 0-436-40989-5*

children's novel   **Andrew Taylor**
The coalhouse
Collins, 1986. ISBN 0-00-184843-7*
Armada, 1987. (pbk). ISBN 0-00-672862-6*
Collins, 1986. (pbk). ISBN 0-00-184844-5*

1987
biography and book of the year   **Christopher Nolan**
Under the eye of the clock
Weidenfeld & Nicolson, 1987.
ISBN 0-297-79092-7*
Isis Large Print Books, 1988.
ISBN 0-15089-266-0*
Pan, 1988. (pbk). ISBN 0-330-30316-3*

Whitbread Literary Awards

novel
: **Ian McEwan**
  The child in time
  Cape, 1987. ISBN 0-224-02499-X*
  Pan, 1988. (pbk). ISBN 0-330-30406-2*

first novel
: **Francis Wyndham**
  The other garden
  Cape, 1987. ISBN 0-224-02475-2*

poetry
: **Seamus Heaney**
  Haw lantern
  Faber & Faber, 1987. ISBN 0-571-14780-1*
  Faber & Faber, 1987. (pbk).
  ISBN 0-571-14781-X*

children's novel
: **Geraldine McCaughrean**
  A little lower than the angels
  Oxford University Press, 1987.
  ISBN 0-19-271561-5*

1988

first novel and book of the year
: **Paul Sayer**
  The comforts of madness
  Constable, 1988. ISBN 0-09-468480-4*
  Hodder & Stoughton, 1989. (pbk).
  ISBN 0-340-50804-3*

novel
: **Salman Rushdie**
  The Satanic verses
  Viking, 1988. ISBN 0-670-82537-9*

biography
: **A. N. Wilson**
  Tolstoy
  Hamish Hamilton, 1988. ISBN 0-241-12190-6*

poetry
: **Peter Porter**
  The automatic order
  Oxford University Press, 1987.
  ISBN 0-19-282088-5*

children's novel
: **Judy Allen**
  Awaiting development
  Julia Macrae, 1988. ISBN 0-86203-356-X*

57 H. H. Wingate Prize

The awards, of £2,000 each, are presented annually for works of fiction and non-fiction which stimulate an interest in and awareness of themes of Jewish concern amongst a wider reading public. Authors must be resident in the UK, Commonwealth, Israel, Pakistan or the Republics of Ireland or South Africa.

Contact   Book Trust
Book House
45 East Hill
London SW18 2QZ
Tel. 01-870 9055

1977
non-fiction   **Chaim Bermant**
Coming home
Allen & Unwin, 1976. ISBN 0-04-920047-X

fiction   **David Markish**
The beginning
Hodder & Stoughton, 1976. ISBN 0-340-18093-5

1978
non-fiction   **Lionel Kochan**
The Jew and his history
Macmillan, 1977. ISBN 0-333-19227-3

fiction   **Dan Jacobson**
Confessions of Josef Baisz
Secker & Warburg, 1977. ISBN 0-436-22045-8

1979
non-fiction   **Nelly Wilson**
Bernard Lazare
Cambridge University Press, 1978.
ISBN 0-521-21802-0

H. H. Wingate Prize

fiction **Emanuel Litvinof**
The face of terror
Michael Joseph, 1978. ISBN 0-7181-1528-7

1980
non-fiction **Lord Nicholas Bethell**
The Palestine triangle: The struggle between the Jews and the Arabs, 1935-1948
Deutsch, 1979. ISBN 0-233-97069-X

fiction **A. B. Yehoshua**
Early in the summer of 1970
Heinemann, 1980. ISBN 0-434-89000-6

1981
non-fiction **Jerry White**
Rothschild buildings: Life in an East End tenement block: 1887-1920
Routledge & Kegan Paul, 1980.
ISBN 0-7100-0603-9*

fiction **Mordecai Richler**
Joshua then and now
Macmillan, 1980. ISBN 0-333-30025-4

1982
non-fiction **David Vital**
Zionism: The formative years
Oxford University Press, 1982.
ISBN 0-19-827443-2*
Oxford University Press, 1988. (pbk).
ISBN 0-19-827715-6*

fiction **T. Carmi**
Penguin book of Hebrew verse
Penguin, 1981. (pbk). ISBN 0-14-042197-1*

Between 1983 and 1985, one prize, which was shared in 1983, was given each year.

H. H. Wingate Prize

1983

Chaim Herzog
The Arab-Israeli wars: War and peace in the Middle East from the War of Independence to Lebanon
Arms and Armour Press, 1984.
ISBN 0-85368-613-0*

Chaim Raphael
The springs of Jewish life
Chatto & Windus, 1983. ISBN 0-7011-2335-4

1984

Naomi Shepherd
Wilfred Israel: German Jewry's secret ambassador
Weidenfeld & Nicolson, 1984.
ISBN 0-297-78308-4*

1985

Yigael Yadin
The Temple scroll: The Hidden law of the Dead Sea Sect
Weidenfeld & Nicolson, 1985.
ISBN 0-297-78411-0*

1986
non-fiction

Conor Cruise O'Brien
The seige: The saga of Zionism and Israel
Weidenfeld & Nicolson, 1986.
ISBN 0-297-78393-9*
Grafton, 1988. (pbk). ISBN 0-586-08645-5*

fiction

David Pryce-Jones
The afternoon sun
Weidenfeld & Nicolson, 1986.
ISBN 0-297-78822-1*

1987
non-fiction

Dan Vittorio Serge
Memoirs of an unfortunate Jew: An Italian story
Halban, 1987. ISBN 1-870015-00-2*
Grafton, 1988. (pbk). ISBN 0-586-08720-6*

H. H. Wingate Prize

fiction
Aharon Appelfeld
The age of wonders
Weidenfeld & Nicolson, 1987.
ISBN 0-297-79155-9*

1988
non-fiction
Anton Gill
The journey back from hell
Grafton, 1988. ISBN 0-246-12897-6*

fiction
Amos Oz
The black box
Chatto & Windus, 1988. ISBN 0-7011-3293-0*
Fontana, 1989. (pbk). ISBN 0-00-654350-2*

58 *Yorkshire Post* Awards

The literary awards, which were founded in 1964, now stand at £1,000 for the Book of the Year, which may be either fiction or non-fiction, and £800 for the Best First Work. The awards for art and music, both worth £500 each, founded in 1981, are for works which have most contributed to the understanding and appreciation of art and music.

Contact
:   Literary Luncheons Officer
    Yorkshire Post
    PO Box 168
    Wellington Street
    Leeds LS1 1RF
    Tel. (0532) 432701 ext. 512

1964
first prize
:   **George Malcolm Thomson**
    The twelve days: 24th July to 4th August 1914
    Sidgwick & Jackson, 1975. ISBN 0-436-50249-6

runner-up
:   **Elizabeth Berridge**
    Across the common
    Heinemann, 1964. BNB B64-17588
    Sphere, 1985. (pbk). ISBN 0-349-10304-6*

1965
first prize
:   **Earl of Birkenhead**
    Halifax
    Hamish Hamilton, 1965. BNB B65-14470

best fiction
:   **Muriel Spark**
    The Mandelbaum gate
    Macmillan, 1965. ISBN 0-333-04142-9*
    Penguin, 1970. (pbk). ISBN 0-14-002745-9*

best first work
:   **Terry Coleman**
    The railway navvies: A history of the men who made the railways
    Penguin, Rev. ed. 1968. BNB B68-10483
    Penguin, 1981. (pbk). ISBN 0-14-005542-8*

Yorkshire Post Awards

1966
first prize — **Rebecca West**
The birds fall down
Macmillan, 1966. BNB B66-20757
Virago, 1986. (pbk). ISBN 0-86068-662-0*

runner-up — **Robert Blake**
Disraeli
Eyre & Spottiswoode, 1966. BNB B66-20883
Methuen, 1969. (pbk). ISBN 0-416-29870-2*

best first work — **Archie Hind**
The dear green place
New Authors, 1966. BNB B66-03373
Polygon Books, 1984. (pbk).
ISBN 0-904919-81-1*

1967
first prize — **Harold Nicolson**
Diaries and letters
Collins, 1967. BNB B67-19306

best fiction — **Laurens van der Post**
The hunter and the whale
Chatto & Windus, 1986. ISBN 0-7011-3043-1*
Penguin, 1970. (pbk). ISBN 0-14-003119-7*

best first work — **Catherine Dupré**
The chicken coop
Geoffrey Blef, 1967

1968
first prize — **Michael Holroyd**
Lytton Strachey
Rev. ed. Heinemann, 1973.
ISBN 0-434-34579-2
New ed. Penguin, 1987. (pbk).
ISBN 0-14-058031-X*

best fiction — **P. H. Newby**
Something to answer for
Faber & Faber, 1968. BNB B68-22011

Yorkshire Post Awards

best first work
J. J. Scarisbrick
Henry VIII
Methuen, 1968. ISBN 0-413-25600-6*
Methuen, 1976. (pbk). ISBN 0-413-36800-9*

runner-up
Sally Trench
Bury me in my boots
Hodder & Stoughton, 1968. ISBN 0-340-02961-7
Hodder & Stoughton, 1983. (pbk).
ISBN 0-340-33332-4*

1969
first prize
Elizabeth Longford
Wellington: The years of the sword
Weidenfeld & Nicolson, 1969.
ISBN 0-297-17917-9*
Panther, 1971. (pbk). ISBN 0-586-03548-6*

best fiction
Iris Murdoch
Bruno's dream
Chatto & Windus, 1969. ISBN 0-7011-1426-6*
Granada, 1977. (pbk). ISBN 0-586-04485-X*
Penguin, 1970. (pbk). ISBN 0-14-003176-6*

best first work
Spike Mays
Ruben's corner: An English country boyhood
Eyre & Spottiswoode, 1969.
ISBN 0-413-27360-1*
Magna Print Books, 1984. (large print ed.).
ISBN 0-86009-580-0*
Robin Clark, 1981. (pbk). ISBN 0-86072-055-1*

runner-up
Eithne Wilkins
The rose garden game: The symbolic background to the European prayer beads
Gollancz, 1969. ISBN 0-575-00224-7

1970

first prize
Angus Wilson
The world of Charles Dickens
Secker & Warburg, 1970. ISBN 0-436-57513-2*
Granada, 1983. (pbk). ISBN 0-586-05816-8*

best fiction
Edna O'Brien
A pagan place
Weidenfeld & Nicolson, 1970.
ISBN 0-297-00027-6*
Isis Large Print Books, 1985.
ISBN 1-85059-055-2*
Penguin, 1971. (pbk). ISBN 0-14-003341-6*

best first work
Patrick Davis
A child at arms
Hutchinson, 1970. ISBN 0-09-102450-1
Buchan & Enright, 1986. (pbk).
ISBN 0-907675-54-9*

runner-up
John M. Carter
The Battle of Actium: The rise and triumph of Augustus Caesar
Hamish Hamilton, 1970. ISBN 0-241-01516-2

1971

first prize
Lord R. A. Butler
The art of the possible: The memoirs of Lord Butler
Hamish Hamilton, 1971. ISBN 0-241-02007-7

best fiction
Paul Scott
Towers of silence
Heinemann, 1971. ISBN 0-434-68110-5*
Chivers Press, 1985. (large print ed.).
ISBN 0-86220-134-9*
Pan, 1988. (pbk). ISBN 0-330-30396-1*

best first work
Lord James Douglas-Hamilton
Motive for a mission: The story of Rudolf Hess's flight to Britain
Macmillan, 1971. ISBN 0-333-12260-7

Yorkshire Post Awards

runner-up   **Stewart Edwards**
The Paris Commune, 1871
Eyre & Spottiswoode, 1971. ISBN 0-413-28110-8

1972
first prize   **Quentin Bell**
Virginia Woolf
Vol. 1. Hogarth Press, 1972. ISBN 0-7012-0291-2
Vol. 2. Hogarth Press, 1972. ISBN 0-7012-0371-4
2 Vols. in 1. Grafton, 1987. (pbk).
ISBN 0-586-08676-5*

best fiction   **Margaret Drabble**
The needle's eye
Weidenfeld & Nicolson, 1972.
ISBN 0-297-99399-2*
Penguin, 1973. (pbk). ISBN 0-14-003666-0*

best first work   **Jennifer Johnston**
The captains and the kings
Hamish Hamilton, 1972. ISBN 0-241-02114-6*
Fontana, 1985. (pbk). ISBN 0-00-654104-6*

runner-up   **Michael Davie**
In the future now: A report from California
Hamish Hamilton, 1972. ISBN 0-241-02181-2

1973
first prize   **Lord David Cecil**
The Cecils of Hatfield House: A portrait of an English ruling family
Constable, 1973. ISBN 0-09-45610-5

best fiction   **Evelyn Anthony**
The occupying power
Hutchinson, 1973. ISBN 0-09-116950-X
Arrow, 1983. (pbk). ISBN 0-09-930320-5*

best first work   **Robin Lane-Fox**
Alexander the Great
Allen Lane, 1973. ISBN 0-7139-0500-X*
Penguin, 1986. (pbk). ISBN 0-14-008878-4*

Yorkshire Post Awards

runner-up **Arianna Stassinopoulos**
The female woman
Davis-Poynter, 1973. ISBN 0-7067-0098-8

1974
first prize **Philip Mason**
A matter of honour: An account of the Indian army, its officers and men
Cape, 1974. ISBN 0-224-00978-8
Papermac, 1986. (pbk). ISBN 0-333-41837-9*

best fiction **Kingsley Amis**
Ending up
Cape, 1974. ISBN 0-224-00988-5*
Penguin, 1987. (pbk). ISBN 0-14-004151-6*

best first work **Anne Redmon**
Emily Stone
Secker & Warburg, 1974. ISBN 0-436-40990-9

runner-up **John Mackinnon**
In search of the red ape
Collins, 1974. ISBN 0-00-216703-4

1975
first prize **Paul Johnston**
Pope John XXIII
Hutchinson, 1975. ISBN 0-09-123790-4

best fiction **David Lodge**
Changing places: A tale of two campuses
Secker & Warburg, 1975. ISBN 0-436-25660-6*
Chivers Press, 1986. (large print ed.)
ISBN 0-7451-7012-9*
Penguin, 1978. (pbk). ISBN 0-14-004656-9*

best first work **Iain and Oria Douglas-Hamilton**
Among the elephants
Collins-Harvill, 1975. ISBN 0-00-262001-4
Collins, 1978. (pbk). ISBN 0-00-370076-3*

runner-up **Sian James**
One afternoon
Peter Davies, 1975. ISBN 0-432-07530-5

1976
first prize **Edward Crankshaw**
The shadow of the Winter Palace
Macmillan, 1977. ISBN 0-333-14882-7*
Papermac, 1986. (pbk). ISBN 0-333-39892-0*

best fiction **Nina Bawden**
The afternoon of a good woman
Macmillan, 1976. ISBN 0-333-21184-7

best first work **Rhoda Edwards**
Some touch of pity
Hutchinson, 1976. ISBN 0-09-125520-1

runner-up **Sasha Moorsom**
A lavender trip
Bodley Head, 1976. ISBN 0-370-10593-1

1977
first prize **Alistair Horne**
A savage war of peace: Algeria 1954–1962
Macmillan, 1977. ISBN 0-333-15515-7*
Macmillan, 1987. (pbk). ISBN 0-333-41398-9*

best fiction **Olivia Manning**
The danger tree
Weidenfeld & Nicolson, 1977.
ISBN 0-297-77296-1*

best first work **Max Egremont**
The cousins: The friendship, opinions and activities of Wilfred Blunt and George Wyndham
Collins, 1977. ISBN 0-00-216134-6

runner-up **John Campbell**
Lloyd George: The goat in wilderness
Cape, 1977. ISBN 0-224-01296-7

1978
first prize **Gavin Kennedy**
Bligh
Duckworth, 1978. ISBN 0-7156-0957-2

Yorkshire Post Awards

best fiction	**Sian James** *Yesterday* Collins, 1978. ISBN 0-00-221959-X
best first work	**Edna Healey** *Lady unknown: The life of Angela Burdett-Coutts* Sidgwick & Jackson, 1978. ISBN 0-283-99162-3
runner-up	**Jane Dunn** *Moon in eclipse: A life of Mary Shelley* Weidenfeld & Nicolson, 1978. ISBN 0-297-77383-6

1979

first prize	**Norman and Jeanne Mackenzie** *Dickens: A life* Oxford University Press, 1979. ISBN 0-19-211741-6
best fiction	**Jennifer Johnston** *The old jest* Hamish Hamilton, 1979. ISBN 0-241-10267-7* G. K. Hall, 1981. (large print ed.). ISBN 0-8161-3091-4* Fontana, 1984. (pbk). ISBN 0-00-654051-1*
best first work	**Mary Soames** *Clementine Churchill* Cassell, 1979. ISBN 0-304-30321-6
runner-up	**Richard Morris** *Cathedrals and abbeys of England and Wales* Dent, 1979. ISBN 0-460-04334-X*

1980

first prize	**Bernard Crick** *George Orwell: A life* Secker & Warburg, Rev. ed. 1981. ISBN 0-436-11451-8 Penguin, 1982. (pbk). ISBN 0-14-005856-7*

Yorkshire Post Awards

best fiction
Anthony Burgess
Earthly powers
Hutchinson, 1980. ISBN 0-09-143910-8
Penguin, 1982. (pbk). ISBN 0-14-005896-6*

best first work
Richard Jenkyns
The Victorians and ancient Greece
Blackwell, 1980. ISBN 0-631-10991-9
Blackwell, 1981. (pbk). ISBN 0-631-12934-0*

runner-up
Sally Emerson
Second sight
Michael Joseph, 1980. ISBN 0-7181-1965-7

1981
first prize
John Julius Norwich
Venice: The greatness and the fall
Allen Lane, 1981. ISBN 0-7139-1409-2

best fiction
Paul Theroux
Mosquito Coast
Hamish Hamilton, 1981. ISBN 0-241-10688-5*

best first work
Francois Kersaudy
Churchill and de Gaulle
Collins, 1981. ISBN 0-00-216328-4*

runner-up
Anthony Seldon
Churchill's Indian summer: The Conservative Government of 1951–1955
Hodder & Stoughton, 1981.
ISBN 0-340-25456-4*

art
Charles Harrison
English art and modernism, 1900–1939
Allen Lane, 1981. ISBN 0-7139-0792-4

music
Charles Osborne
The complete operas of Puccini
Gollancz, 1981. ISBN 0-575-03013-5*
De Capo Press, 1983. (pbk).
ISBN 0-306-80200-7*

225

Yorkshire Post Awards

1982

first prize
: **John Mortimer**
  Clinging to the wreckage: A part of life
  Weidenfeld & Nicolson, 1982.
  ISBN 0-297-76010-7
  Penguin, 1983. (pbk). ISBN 0-14-006383-8*

best fiction
: **Elizabeth Jane Howard**
  Getting it right
  Hamish Hamilton, 1982. ISBN 0-241-10805-5*
  Ulverscroft Large Print Books, 1983.
  ISBN 0-7089-8140-2*
  Penguin, 1976. (pbk). ISBN 0-14-004138-9*

best first work
: **Sir David Fraser**
  Alanbrooke
  Collins, 1982. ISBN 0-00-216360-8

runner-up
: **Dan van der Vat**
  The grand scuttle: The sinking of the German fleet at Scapa Flow in 1919
  Maritime Books, 1985. ISBN 0-86228-099-0*
  Grafton, 1988. (pbk). ISBN 0-586-20091-6*

art
: **Hugh Honour and John Fleming**
  A world history of art
  Macmillan, 1982. ISBN 0-333-23583-5
  Papermac, 1984. (pbk). ISBN 0-333-37185-2*

music
: **William Mann**
  James Galway's music in time
  Mitchell Beazley, 1982. ISBN 0-85533-382-0

1983

first prize
: **Max Hastings and Simon Jenkins**
  Battle for the Falklands
  Michael Joseph, 1983. ISBN 0-7181-2228-3

best fiction
: **Francis King**
  Act of darkness
  Hutchinson, 1982. ISBN 0-09-153520-4
  Ulverscroft Large Print Books, 1984.
  ISBN 0-7089-8207-7*

biography of the year	**Kenneth Rose** *King George V* Weidenfeld & Nicolson, 1983. ISBN 0-297-78245-2 Papermac, 1984. (pbk). ISBN 0-333-37224-7*
best first work	**Richard Lamb** *Montgomery in Europe 1943–1945: Success or failure?* Buchan & Enright, 1983. ISBN 0-907675-04-2 Buchan & Enright, 1987. (pbk). ISBN 0-907675-77-8*
runner-up	**Richard Masefield** *Chalkhill Blue* Heinemann, 1983. ISBN 0-434-45260-2 Ulverscroft Large Print Books, 1985. ISBN 0-7089-1269-9* Pan, 1984. (pbk). ISBN 0-330-28397-9*
art	**Susan Beattie** *The new sculpture* Yale University Press, 1983. ISBN 0-300-02860-1* Yale University Press, 1984. (pbk). ISBN 0-300-03359-1*
music	**Alan Walker** *Franz Liszt: The virtuoso years* Faber & Faber, 1983. ISBN 0-571-10568-8*

1984

first prize	**Max Hastings** *Overlord: D-Day and the battle for Normandy* Michael Joseph, 1984. ISBN 0-7181-2326-3 Pan, 1985. (pbk). ISBN 0-330-29691-9*
novel of the year	**Kingsley Amis** *Stanley and the women* Hutchinson, 1984. Penguin, 1985. (pbk). ISBN 0-14-007607-7*
best first work	**Michael Parnell** *Eric Linklater: A critical biography* John Murray, 1984. ISBN 0-7195-4109-3*

Yorkshire Post Awards

runner-up	**James Buchan** *A parish of rich women* Hamish Hamilton, 1984. ISBN 0-241-11310-5* Futura, 1987. (pbk). ISBN 0-7088-3370-5*
art	**David Hill** *In Turner's footsteps: Through the hills and dales of Northern England* John Murray, 1984. ISBN 0-7195-4149-2*
music	**Christopher Hogwood** *Handel* Thames and Hudson, 1984. ISBN 0-500-01355-1* Thames and Hudson, 1988. (pbk). ISBN 0-500-27498-3*

1985

first prize	**John Terraine** *The right of the line* Hamish Hamilton, 1985. ISBN 0-340-26644-9* Sceptre, 1988. (pbk). ISBN 0-340-41919-9*
novel of the year	**Alice Thomas Ellis** *Unexplained laughter* Duckworth, 1985. ISBN 0-7156-2070-3* Penguin, 1986. (pbk). ISBN 0-14-009203-X*
best first work	**John David Morley** *Pictures from the water trade: An Englishman in Japan* Deutsch, 1985. ISBN 0-233-97703-1* Fontana, 1986. (pbk). ISBN 0-00-654146-1*
runner-up	**Patricia Angadi** *The governess* Gollancz, 1985. ISBN 0-575-03485-8* Corgi, 1986. (pbk). ISBN 0-552-99201-1*
art	**Lord Thorneycroft** *The amateur: A companion to water colour* Sidgwick & Jackson, 1985. ISBN 0-283-99246-8* Sidgwick & Jackson, 1986. (pbk). ISBN 0-383-99318-9*

Yorkshire Post Awards

music   **Denis Matthews**
               Beethoven
               Dent, 1985. ISBN 0-460-03178-3*
               Dent, 1987. (pbk). ISBN 0-283-99318-9*

1986
book of the year **Robert Rhodes James**
                  Anthony Eden
                  Weidenfeld & Nicolson, 1986.
                  ISBN 0-297-78979-9*
                  Papermac, 1987. (pbk). ISBN 0-333-45503-7*

best first work   **John Charmley**
                  Duff Cooper: The authorised biography
                  Weidenfeld & Nicolson, 1986.
                  ISBN 0-297-78857-4*
                  Papermac, 1987. (pbk). ISBN 0-333-42823-4*

art   **Paul Hogarth**
                  The artist as reporter
                  Gordon Fraser, 1986. ISBN 0-86092-084-4*

music   **Malcolm Boyd**
                  Domenico Scarlatti: Master of music
                  Weidenfeld & Nicolson, 1986.
                  ISBN 0-297-78997-X*

1987
book of the year **Lyn Macdonald**
                  1914
                  Michael Joseph, 1987. ISBN 0-7181-2394-8*
                  Penguin, 1989. (pbk). ISBN 0-14-011651-6*

best first work   **Anne Spillard**
                  The cartomancer
                  Hamish Hamilton, 1988. ISBN 0-241-12345-3*

art   **James King**
                  Interior landscapes: Biography of Paul Nash
                  Weidenfeld & Nicolson, 1987.
                  ISBN 0-297-7908-1*

Yorkshire Post Awards

music **Winton Dean and John Merrill**
Handel's operas, 1704 – 1726
Oxford University Press, 1987.
ISBN 0-19-315219-3*

NEW PRIZES

Ian St James Awards

The awards, set up in 1989 by the thriller writer Ian St James, are for 12 previously unpublished short stories which will be published by Collins. The prize money of £28,000, provided by the author himself, will make the awards the richest for fiction in the UK.

The first awards were announced in September 1989 which was too late for inclusion in this book.

Contact   Collins Sons & Co. Ltd.
8 Grafton Street
London W1X 3LA
Tel. 01-493 7070

P. G. Wodehouse Prize

The prize of £5,000 and publication by Century Hutchinson is for the best unpublished comic work of fiction or non-fiction.

The first prize was awarded late in 1989 which was too late for inclusion in this book.

Contact   Century Hutchinson
Brookmount House
62 – 65 Chandos Place
London WC2N 4NW
Tel. 01-240 3411

Author Index

Introduction
Authors are listed alphabetically below along with a shortened title and date of the prize(s) or award(s) which they have won in chronological order. Shortlisted authors are indicated by 'SL' after the prize name. The index may be used to trace works of favourite authors which have won awards or to trace their success over the years.

The sample entry listed below charts the career of Jeanette Winterson who won the Whitbread First Novel Award in 1985 and the John Llewellyn Rhys Memorial Prize in 1987. To find out her winning titles the lists for each prize would have to be consulted.

    Winterson, Jeanette   Whitbread (1985), Rhys (1987)

A list of the shortened titles of the prizes and awards follows:

Ackerley	J. R. Ackerley Prize
Angel	Angel Literary Prize
Authors	Author's Club First Novel Award
Bartlett	Alice Hunt Bartlett Award
Bejam	Bejam Cookery Book of the Year
BFI	British Film Institute Book Award
Black	James Tait Black Memorial Prizes
Boardman	Boardman Tasker Memorial Award for Mountain Literature
Booker	Booker Prize
Cheltenham	Cheltenham Prize
Clarke	Arthur C. Clarke Award
Collins	Collins Religious Book Award
Commonwealth	Commonwealth Writers' Prize
Constable	Constable Trophy
Cook	Thomas Cook Travel and Guide Book Awards
Cooper	Duff Cooper Memorial Prize
CWA	Crime Writers' Association Awards
Davies	Hunter Davies Prize for the Lakeland Book of the Year
Elgin	Mary Elgin Award
Express	*Sunday Express* Book of the Year
Faber	Geoffrey Faber Memorial Prize
Fawcett	Fawcett Society Book Prize
Guardian	*Guardian* Fiction Prize

Author Index

Hawthornden	Hawthornden Prize
Higham	David Higham Prize for Fiction
Historical	Historical Novel Prize in Memory of Georgette Heyer
Holtby	Winifred Holtby Memorial Prize
Hurst	Nelson Hurst and Marsh Biography Award
Kent	Sir Peter Kent Conservation Book Prize
King	King George's Fund for Sailors Book of the Sea Award
London	London Tourist Board Guide Book of the Year Awards
Machell	Roger Machell Prize
Mackenzie	Mackenzie Prize
McVities	McVitie's Prize for the Scottish Writer of the Year
Maugham	Somerset Maugham Award
MIND	MIND Book of the Year
NCR	NCR Book Award for Non-Fiction
Odd	Odd Fellows (Manchester Unity) Social Concern Book Award
Pen	Silver Pen Awards
Portico	Portico Prize
Rhys	John Llewellyn Rhys Memorial Prize
RNA	Romantic Novelists Association Awards
RSL	Royal Society of Literature Award under the W. H. Heinemann Bequest
Runciman	Runciman Award
SAC	Scottish Arts Council Book Awards
Saltire	Saltire Society and *The Scotsman* Literary Award
Science	Science Book Prize
SCSE	SCSE Book Prizes
Simon	André Simon Memorial Fund Book Awards
Smith	W. H. Smith Literary Award
Southern	Southern Arts Literature Prize
Stanford	Winifred Mary Stanford Prize
Trask	Betty Trask Awards
TSB	TSB Peninsula Prize
WAC	Welsh Arts Council Awards
Whitbread	Whitbread Literary Awards
Wingate	H. H. Wingate Prize
YP	*Yorkshire Post* Awards

Author Index

Abse, Dannie	WAC (1971, 1980 & 1987)
Acaster, Linda	RNA (1986)
Achebe, Chinua	Booker SL (1987)
Acherson, Neal	Saltire (1988)
Ackerley, J. R.	Smith (1962)
Ackroyd, Peter	Maugham, RSL & Whitbread (1984), Guardian & Whitbread (1985), Booker SL (1987)
Adair, Gilbert	Authors (1988)
Adamson, Edward	MIND (1984)
Aldington, R.	Black (1946)
Aldridge, Alan	Whitbread (1973)
Aldridge, James	Rhys (1945)
Alexander, Patrick	CWA (1976)
Allen, Judy	Whitbread (1988)
Allerton, Jay	RNA (1975)
Allsop, Kenneth	Rhys (1950)
Ambler, Eric	CWA (1959, 1967 & 1972)
Amis, Kingsley	Maugham (1955), Booker SL & YP (1974), Booker SL (1978), YP (1984), Booker (1986)
Amis, Martin	Maugham (1974)
Anderson, R. D.	SAC (1984)
Anderson, William	Pen (1981)
Andrewes, Georgina	Trask SL (1988)
Angadi, Patricia	YP SL (1985)
Annan, Noel G.	Black (1951)
Anthony, Evelyn	YP (1973)
Appelfeld, Aharon	Wingate (1987)
Arden, John	Booker SL (1982)
Armitage, Gary	Trask SL (1985)
Arnold, Catherine	Trask SL (1987)
Arnold, Eric	Odd (1982)
Ash, Timothy Garton	Maugham (1984)
Ashby, M. K.	Black (1961)
Ashworth, Elizabeth	Bartlett (1975)
Athill, Diana	Ackerley (1987)
Atwood, Margaret	Booker SL & Clarke (1986)
Automobile Association	Davies (1984)
Bailey, Paul	Authors (1967), Maugham (1968), Booker SL (1977 & 1986)

Author Index

Bainbridge, Beryl	Booker SL (1973), Booker SL & Guardian (1974), Whitbread (1977)
Baines, Chris	Kent (1987)
Baines, Jocelyn	Cooper (1961)
Baker, J. A.	Cooper (1967)
Ball, John	CWA (1966)
Ball, Stephen	SCSE (1987)
Ballard, J. G.	Black, Booker SL & Guardian (1984)
Banks, Iain	SAC (1987)
Bantock, G. H.	SCSE (1984)
Bantock, Gavin	Bartlett (1966)
Banville, John	Black (1976), Guardian (1981)
Barber, Richard William	Maugham (1971)
Barker, A. L.	Maugham (1947), Booker SL (1970), Pen (1988)
Barker, Pat	Fawcett (1983)
Barnes, Julian	Maugham (1981), Booker SL (1984), Faber (1985)
Barrington, John	SAC (1985)
Barrow, Geoffrey W. S.	SAC (1981)
Barry, Clive	Guardian (1965)
Batchelor, Stephen	Cook (1988)
Battiscombe, Georgina	Black (1963)
Bawden, Nina	YP (1976), Booker SL (1987)
Beattie, N.	SCSE (1985)
Beattie, Susan	YP (1983)
Belfrage, Nicholas	Simon (1985)
Bell, A.	SCSE (1987)
Bell, Quentin	Black, Cooper & YP (1972)
Bennett, Alan	Hawthornden (1989)
Bennett, Arnold	Black (1923)
Bennett, Margot	Cooper (1958)
Benson, Barbara	Authors (1977)
Benson, Peter	Authors, Guardian & Trask (1987)
Bentley, James	Cook (1988)
Berger, John	Black, Booker & Guardian (1972)
Bermant, Chaim	Wingate (1977)
Bernlef, J.	MIND (1988)
Berridge, Elizabeth	YP SL (1964)
Bethell, Lord Nicholas	Wingate (1980)
Betjeman, John	Cooper (1958)
Bevan, Ian	Machell (1987)
Bhabra, H. S.	Trask SL (1987)
Bhatt, Sujata	Bartlett (1987)

Author Index

Bigood, Ruth — WAC (1976)
Bilcliffe, Roger — SAC (1986)
Birch, Carol — Higham (1988)
Birkenhead, Earl of — YP (1965)
Blackwood, Caroline — Higham (1976), Booker SL (1977)
Blake, Kathryn — RNA (1988)
Blake, Philippa — Trask SL (1986)
Blake, Quentin — Whitbread (1974)
Blake, Robert — YP SL (1966)
Bloom, Harry — Authors (1956)
Blount, Margaret — Guardian (1970)
Blunden, Edmund — Hawthornden (1922)
Blythe, Ronald — Angel (1986)
Boardman, Peter — Rhys (1979)
Bond, Ruskin — Rhys (1957)
Bonfiglioli, Kyril — CWA (1973)
Boston, Sarah — Odd (1981)
Bowen, Carol — Bejam (1984)
Bowen, Elizabeth — Black (1969), Booker SL (1970)
Boyd, Malcolm — YP (1986)
Boyd, William — Whitbread (1981), Booker SL, Maugham & Rhys (1982), Express SL (1987), SAC (1988)
Boyle, Andrew — Whitbread (1974)
Bradbury, Malcolm — RSL (1975), Booker SL (1983)
Bragg, Melvyn — Rhys (1969), Pen (1970)
Brason, Gill — Odd (1978)
Brent, Madeleine — RNA (1978)
Brink, André — Booker SL (1976 & 1978)
British Medical Association — Science (1988)
Bromwich, Rachel — WAC (1983)
Brook, Stephen — Simon (1987)
Brooke-Rose, Christine — Black (1966)
Brookner, Anita — Booker (1984)
Brooks, John — Cook (1980)
Brown, Francis Yeats — Black (1930)
Brown, George Mackay — SAC (1984), Black (1987)
Brown, Malcolm — NCR (1989)
Bryson, John — CWA (1986)
Buchan, James — Higham, Trask SL, Whitbread & YP SL (1984)
Buchan, John — Black (1928)
Buey, Christof — Bejam (1988)

Author Index

Burgess, Anthony	Booker SL & YP (1980), Ackerley (1987)
Burnett, John	Odd (1984)
Burnside, John	SAC (1988)
Burns, Jimmy	Maugham (1988)
Burton, Jack	Stanford (1978)
Bush, Duncan	WAC (1984 & 1986)
Butler, Gwendoline	CWA (1973), RNA (1981)
Butler, Lord R. A.	YP (1971)
Butlin, Ron	SAC (1983, 1984 & 1985)
Byatt, A. S.	Pen (1986)
Caird, George B.	Collins (1981)
Calder, Angus	Rhys (1970), SAC (1982)
Calder, Nigel	King (1986)
Camberton, Roland	Maugham (1951)
Cameron, David Kerr	SAC (1981)
Cameron, John Kerr	SAC (1985)
Campbell, Beatrix	Cheltenham (1984), Fawcett (1988)
Campbell, John	YP SL (1977)
Canning, Victor	CWA (1972)
Carey, Peter	Booker SL (1985), Booker (1988)
Carluccio, Antonio	Bejam (1987)
Carmi, P.	Wingate (1982)
Carpenter, Humphrey	Maugham (1980), Cooper (1988)
Carr, J. L.	Booker SL & Guardian (1980), Booker SL (1985)
Carter, Angela	Rhys (1968), Maugham (1969), Cheltenham (1979), Black (1984)
Carter, John M.	YP SL (1970)
Cartwright, Justin	Express SL (1988)
Cary, Joyce	Black (1941)
Cash, Jonathan	CWA (1977)
Cave, Julia	NCR (1989)
Caute, David	Authors (1959), Rhys (1960)
Cecil, Lord David	Black & Hawthornden (1929), YP (1973)
Chambers, Sir Edmund	Black (1938)
Chambers, Frederick R. Hyde	Authors (1984)
Chambers, R. W.	Black (1935)
Charles, Gerda	Black (1963), Whitbread (1971)
Charmley, John	YP (1986)
Chatwin, Bruce	Hawthornden (1977), Black & Whitbread (1982), Booker SL (1988)
Chaudhuri, Nirad C.	Cooper (1966), NCR SL (1988)

Author Index

Checkland, Olive	SAC (1981)
Chisholm, Anne	Pen (1980)
Christiansen, Rupert	Maugham (1989)
Ciment, Michael	BFI (1986)
Clancy, Joseph P.	WAC (1971)
Clare, George	Smith (1982)
Clarke, Ethne	Angel (1988)
Clarke, Gillian	WAC (1979)
Clayton, Sylvia	Guardian (1975)
Clemeau, Carol	CWA (1983)
Clifford, Francis	CWA (1969 & 1974)
Clifton, Violet	Black (1933)
Cobb, Richard Charles	Ackerley (1984)
Cody, Liza	CWA (1980)
Coetzee, J. M.	Black (1980), Faber (1981), Booker (1983)
Colegate, Isabel	Smith (1981)
Coleman, Terry	YP (1965)
Compton-Burnett, Ivy	Black (1955)
Connell, John	Black (1949)
Conrad, Peter	Machell (1988)
Constantine, David	Bartlett (1983), Runciman (1986), Southern (1988)
Cook, David	Hawthornden (1978), Southern (1984)
Cooper, Dominic	Maugham (1976)
Corbett, W. J.	Whitbread (1982)
Cork, Richard	Rhys (1977)
Corke, Helen	Whitbread (1975)
Cornwell, John	CWA (1982)
Corrigan, Felicitas	Black (1986)
Coulton, G. G.	Black (1943)
Cowan, Ian	SAC (1983)
Crace, Jim	Guardian, Higham & Whitbread (1986)
Crampsey, Robert A.	SAC (1981)
Crankshaw, Edward	YP (1976), Whitbread (1982)
Cranston, Maurice	Black (1957)
Crawford, Alan	Cooper (1986)
Cremer, Peter	King SL (1984)
Crick, Bernard	YP (1980)
Croll, P.	SCSE (1985)
Crossley, Rosemary	MIND (1982)
Crowther, Geoff	Cook (1982)
Crozier, Andrew	Bartlett (1976)
Cruikshank, Edward	RSL (1976)

Author Index

Cunliffe, Tom	King (1988)
Dahl, Roald	Whitbread (1983)
Daiches, David	Saltire (1984)
Davidson, Lionel	Authors & CWA (1960), CWA (1966 & 1978)
Davidson, Robyn	Cook (1980)
Davie, Elspeth	SAC (1985)
Davie, Michael	YP SL (1972)
Davies, Dick	RSL (1980)
Davies, John	Bartlett (1985)
Davies, Robertson	Booker SL (1986)
Davies, Tom	Stanford (1986)
Davis, Patrick	YP (1970)
Dawkins, Richard	RSL (1986)
Dawson, Jennifer	Black (1961)
Dayus, Kathleen	Ackerley (1983)
Dean, Winton	YP (1987)
Dennis, Geoffrey	Hawthornden (1930)
Desai, Anita	Holtby (1977), Booker SL (1980 & 1984)
Dexter, Colin	CWA (1979 & 1981)
Dibdin, Michael	CWA (1988)
Dickinson, Peter	CWA (1968 & 1969), Whitbread (1979)
Dodd, C. H.	Collins (1971)
Dodds, Eric Robertson	Cooper (1977)
Donaldson, Gordon	SAC (1984)
Donnelly, Morwena	Rhys (1943)
Douglas, David C.	Black (1939)
Douglas-Hamilton, Iain	YP (1975)
Douglas-Hamilton, Lord James	YP (1971)
Douglas-Hamilton, Oria	YP (1975)
Douglas-Home, Robin	Authors (1964)
Drabble, Margaret	Rhys (1966), Black (1967), YP (1972)
Duffy, Carol Ann	SAC (1986), Maugham (1988)
Dunbar, Catherine	Elgin (1981)
Dunlop, Eileen	SAC (1983 & 1986)
Dunmore, Helen	Bartlett (1986)
Dunn, Douglas	Maugham (1972), Faber (1976), Hawthornden (1981), SAC & Whitbread (1985)
Dunn, Jane	YP SL (1978)
Dunn, Nell	Rhys (1964)
Dupre, Catherine	YP (1967)

Author Index

Durrell, Lawrence	Cooper (1957), Black (1974), Booker SL (1982)
Dutton, G. F.	SAC (1987)
Earle, Jean	WAC (1981)
Ecclestone, Alan	Collins (1975)
Edgar, Josephine	RNA (1979)
Edmonds, Mark	London (1988)
Edric, Robert	Black (1985)
Edwards, Rhoda	YP (1976)
Edwards, Ruth Dudley	Black (1987)
Edwards, Stewart	YP SL (1971)
Egremont, Max	YP (1977)
Elliot, Charles	Collins (1985)
Elliott, Janice	Southern (1981)
Ellis, Alice Thomas	WAC (1978), Booker SL (1982), WAC (1983), YP (1985)
Ellman, Lucy	Guardian (1988)
Ellman, Richard	Black & Cooper (1982)
Emerson, Sally	YP SL (1980)
England, Barry	Authors (1968), Booker SL (1969)
England, Richard	King (1981)
Ervine, St John Greer	Black (1956)
Evans, Christopher	Odd (1980)
Evans, Margaret	Elgin (1980)
Evans, Paul	Bartlett (1972)
Evans, Stuart	WAC (1978)
Everett, Peter	Maugham (1965)
Fairbairns, Zoe	Fawcett (1985)
Fairbrother, Nan	Smith (1971)
Farrell, J. G.	Faber (1971), Booker (1973)
Feiling, Keith	Black (1954)
Fell, Alison	Bartlett (1984)
Fenton, James	Southern (1981), Faber (1984)
Ferguson, Patricia	Higham (1985), Maugham & Trask (1986)
Fermor, Patrick Leigh	Cooper (1959), Smith (1978), Cook (1986/7), Pen (1987)
Ferris, Paul	WAC (1978)
Field, Frank	Odd (1978)
Fielding, Gabriel	Smith (1962)
Figes, Eva	Guardian (1967)
Fine, Anne	SAC (1986)

Author Index

Finlayson, Geoffrey	SAC (1982)
Finney, Brian	Black (1979)
Finney, Patricia	Higham (1977)
Fisher, Alan	Historical (1984)
Fisher, Allen	Bartlett (1974)
Fisher, Bob	King (1984)
Fisher, H. A. L.	Black (1927)
Fisher, Richard B.	Cook (1989)
Fitzgerald, Penelope	Booker SL (1978), Booker (1979), Booker SL (1988)
Fitzgerald, Valerie	Historical (1981), RNA (1982)
Fleetwood, Hugh	Rhys (1974)
Fleming, Joan	CWA (1962 & 1970)
Fleming, John	YP (1982)
Flint, Helen	Trask (1987)
Fontana/Hachette	Cook (1987)
Forester, C. S.	Black (1938)
Forster, E. M.	Black (1924)
Fothergill, Brian	Pen (1970), RSL (1979)
Fowles, John	Pen (1969), Smith (1970)
Fox, Adam	Black (1960)
Fox, Robin Lane-	Black, Cooper & YP (1973)
Frame, Ronald	Trask (1984), SAC (1985 & 1987)
Francis, Dick	CWA (1979)
Fraser, Lady Antonia	Black (1969)
Fraser, Sir David	YP (1982)
Fraser, Eugenie	SAC (1985)
Frayn, Michael	Maugham (1966), Hawthornden (1967)
Freeman, John	Hawthornden (1920)
French, Edith	Constable (1984)
French, Ilva	London (1986)
Friel, James	Trask SL (1988)
Fuller, John	Faber (1974), Southern (1980), Booker SL & Whitbread (1983)
Fuller, Roy	Cooper (1968)
Furlong, Monica	Stanford (1982)
Gage, Nicholas	RSL (1983)
Gallacher, Tom	SAC (1983 & 1986)
Gant, Phyllis	Elgin (1973)
Ganzl, Kurt	Machell (1987)
Gardam, Jane	Higham & Holtby (1975), Booker SL (1978), Whitbread (1981)
Gardner, P.	SCSE (1984)

Garfield, Leon	Whitbread (1980)
Garlick, Raymond	WAC (1969, 1973, 1977)
Garnett, Angelica	Ackerley (1985)
Garnett, David	Black (1922), Hawthornden (1923)
Garside, Evelyn	Cook (1981)
Gaskell, Jane	Maugham (1970)
Gee, Maurice	Black (1978)
George, Rosemary	Simon (1984)
George, Sara	CWA (1975)
Gerin, Winifred	Black (1967), Whitbread (1976)
Gilbert, Anne	RNA (1976)
Gilbert, Jay	Elgin (1971)
Gill, Anton	Wingate (1988)
Gill, B. M.	CWA (1984)
Gill, Linda	Boardman (1984)
Gillies, Valerie	SAC (1985)
Girouard, Mark	Cooper (1978), Smith (1979)
Gittings, Robert	Smith (1969), Black (1978), Southern (1986)
Glendinning, Victoria	Black & Cooper (1981), Whitbread (1983)
Godden, Rumer	Whitbread (1972)
Golding, William	Black (1979), Booker (1980)
Gombrich, Ernest H.	Smith (1964)
Gordimer, Nadine	Smith (1961), Black (1971), Booker SL (1973)
Gordon, Katharine	Authors & Elgin (1978)
Gordon, Lyndall	Black (1984)
Gore, John	Black (1941)
Gosling, Paula	CWA (1978 & 1985)
Gould, Tony	Pen (1984)
Goulden, Margery	RNA (1979)
Graham, Winston	CWA (1955)
Graves, Robert	Black (1934), Hawthornden (1935)
Gray, Alisdair	SAC (1981), Saltire (1982), Cheltenham & SAC (1983)
Gray, Simon	Cheltenham (1982)
Green, Henrietta	Simon (1987)
Greene, Graham	Hawthornden (1941), Black (1948), Express SL (1988)
Greenleaf, W. H.	Mackenzie (1987)
Gregory, Stephen	Maugham & WAC (1987)
Grieg, J. Y. T.	Black (1931)
Grierson, Edward	CWA (1956)

Author Index

Griffiths, Bill	Bartlett (1974)
Grigg, John	Whitbread (1978)
Grigson, Geoffrey	Cooper (1971), Southern (1985)
Grigson, Jane	Simon (1982)
Gross, John	Cooper (1969)
Guest, Lynn	Historical (1980)
Gunn, Neil M.	Black (1937)
Gunn, Thom	Maugham (1959), Smith (1980)
Gwynn, Stephen	Black (1932)
Haight, Gordon S.	Black (1968)
Hall, Radycliffe	Black (1926)
Hamilton, Nigel	Whitbread (1981)
Hanley, James	WAC (1979)
Hardwick, Mollie	RNA (1977)
Hardy, Denis	Angel (1985)
Hardy, Phil	BFI (1984)
Hardy, Ronald	Black (1962), Express SL (1987)
Hardyment, Christina	Davies (1985)
Hare, David	Rhys (1975)
Hargreaves, David H.	SCSE (1982/3)
Harriot, Ted	Higham (1980)
Harris, Helen	Trask SL (1984), Authors (1986)
Harrison, Charles	YP (1981)
Harrison, Tony	Faber (1972)
Harsent, David	Faber (1978)
Hart, Francis Russell	SAC (1982)
Hartley, L. P.	Black (1947)
Harvey, John	Higham (1979)
Harvey, Samantha	RNA (1981)
Harwood, Lee	Bartlett (1976)
Hassall, Christopher	Hawthornden (1939), Black (1959)
Hastings, Max	Maugham (1980), YP (1983 & 1984), NCR SL (1988)
Hastings, Michael	Maugham (1971)
Hastings, Miriam	MIND (1987)
Hawking, Stephen	NCR (1989)
Haworth, Don	Portico (1986)
Hayman, S. T.	CWA (1982)
Haywood, Trevor	Davies (1986/7)
Healey, Edna	YP (1978)
Healy, John	Ackerley (1989)
Heaney, Seamus	Faber & Maugham (1968), Cooper (1975), Smith (1976), Whitbread (1987)

Author Index

Hearne, John	Rhys (1956)
Heath, Roy A. K.	Guardian (1978)
Heiney, Paul	King (1985)
Hemingway, Maggie	Holtby (1986)
Hemlow, Joyce	Black (1958)
Henderson, Hamish	Maugham (1949)
Hendry, Frances Mary	SAC (1987)
Henriquez, Robert	Black (1950)
Herbert, Kathleen	Historical (1983)
Herley, Richard	Holtby (1978)
Herzog, Chaim	Wingate (1983)
Higgins, Aidan	Black (1966)
Highsmith, Patricia	CWA (1964)
Hill, Christopher	RSL (1977)
Hill, David	YP (1984)
Hill, Geoffrey	Hawthornden (1969), Faber (1970), Bartlett & Whitbread (1971), Cooper (1979)
Hill, Susan	Maugham (1971), Booker SL, Rhys & Whitbread (1972)
Hillman, Ellis	London (1985)
Hilton, James	Hawthornden (1934)
Hind, Archie	Guardian & YP (1966)
Hingley, Ronald	Black (1976)
Hoban, Russell	Whitbread (1974)
Hodgman, Helen	Maugham (1979)
Hofman, Michael	Faber (1988)
Hogan, Desmond	Rhys (1980)
Hogarth, Paul	YP (1986)
Hogwood, Christopher	YP (1984)
Hollinghurst, Alan	Maugham (1989)
Holloway, Richard	Stanford (1984)
Holmes, Richard	Maugham (1977)
Holroyd, Michael	YP (1968)
Holtby, Winifred	Black (1936)
Honour, Hugh	YP (1982)
Hood, Stuart	Saltire (1986)
Hooker, Jeremy	WAC (1975)
Hooker, Susan	Odd (1977)
Hope, Annette	SAC (1988)
Hope, Christopher	Higham (1981), Pen (1983), Whitbread (1984)
Horne, Alistair	Hawthornden (1963), YP (1977)
Horse, Harry	SAC (1984)

Author Index

Hough, Richard	King (1972)
Houghton, Paul	Trask (1989)
Houston, Douglas	WAC (1987)
Howard, Audrey	RNA (1988)
Howard, Elizabeth Jane	Rhys (1951), YP (1982)
Howard, Mary	RNA (1980)
Howard, Michael	Cooper (1962)
Howker, Janni	Whitbread (1985), Maugham (1987)
Hughes, David	Smith & WAC (1985)
Hughes, Gerald W.	Collins (1987)
Hughes, Glyn	Guardian & Higham (1982)
Hughes, M.	SCSE (1986)
Hughes, Robert	Cooper (1987), Smith (1988)
Hughes, Ted	Maugham (1960), Hawthornden (1961), RSL (1979)
Hulme, Keri	Booker (1985)
Hume, John R.	Simon (1981)
Humphries, Emyr	Maugham (1953), WAC (1972, 1975, 1979 & 1984)
Hunter, James	SAC (1986)
Hunter, Jim	Authors (1961)
Huntford, Roland	Hurst (1987)
Hutchinson, R. C.	Smith (1966), Booker SL (1976)
Hutton, John	CWA (1983)
Huxley, Aldous	Black (1939)
Hyde, Paul	SAC (1986)
Hyland, Paul	Bartlett (1984)
Ibbotson, Eva	RNA (1983)
Ignatieff, Michael	RSL (1987), NCR SL (1988)
Ihimaera, Witti	Commonwealth SL (1987)
Ingalls, Rachel	Authors (1970)
Ingoldby, Grace	Southern (1987)
Ironside, Elizabeth	CWA (1984), Elgin & Trask SL (1985)
Ishiguro, Kazuo	Holtby (1982), Booker SL & Whitbread (1986)
Iyayi, Festus	Commonwealth (1988)
Jack, Ian	SAC (1988)
Jacobson, Dan	Rhys (1959), Maugham (1964), Wingate (1978), Ackerley (1986)
Jagger, Brenda	RNA (1986)
James, Naomi	King (1987)
James, P. D.	CWA (1971, 1975 & 1986)

Author Index

James, Robert Rhodes	Rhys (1962), YP (1986)
James, Sian	WAC (1984), YP SL (1975), YP (1978)
Jameson, Storm	Pen (1973/4)
Jamie, Kathleen	SAC (1983 & 1988)
Japrisot, Sebastian	CWA (1968)
Jarman, Rosemary Hawley	Authors (1971)
Jeal, Tim	Rhys (1975)
Jenkins, Mike	WAC (1984)
Jenkins, Simon	YP (1983)
Jenkyns, Richard	YP (1980)
Jennings, Elizabeth	Maugham (1956), Smith (1987)
Jhabvala, Ruth Prawer	Booker (1975)
Johnson, B. S.	Maugham (1967)
Johnson, Hugh	Simon (1983)
Johnston, Jennifer	YP (1972), Authors (1973/4), Booker SL (1977), Whitbread & YP (1979)
Johnston, Paul	YP (1975)
Jones, David Michael	Hawthornden (1938)
Jones, Gareth	Trask SL (1984)
Jones, Glyn	WAC (1969)
Jones, Henry Festing	Black (1919)
Jones, Mary	WAC (1986)
Jones, R. Merfyn	WAC (1982)
Jones, Richard	WAC (1972)
Jones, Sally Roberts	WAC (1970)
Jones, Tristan	WAC (1979)
Jordan, Neil	Guardian (1979)
Joseph, Jenny	Black (1986)
Joseph, Marie	RNA (1987)
Joubert, Elsa	Holtby (1980)
Judd, Alan	Holtby (1981)
Karn, Valerie	Odd (1977)
Kavanagh, P. J.	Guardian (1968)
Kay, Susan	Historical & Trask (1985)
Keane, Molly	Booker SL (1981), Pen (1989)
Keates, Jonathan	Black & Hawthornden (1983)
Keating, H. R. F.	CWA (1964 & 1980)
Kelly, Mary	CWA (1961)
Kelman, James	SAC (1983), Cheltenham & SAC (1987)
Keneally, Thomas	Booker SL (1972, 1975 & 1979), Booker (1982)
Kennedy, Gavin	YP (1978)

Kennedy, Margaret	Black (1953)
Kersaudy, Francois	YP (1981)
Kesson, Jessie	SAC (1986)
Ketton-Cremer, R. W.	Black (1955)
Keyes, Sidney	Hawthornden (1943)
Keynes, Geoffrey	Black (1966)
Khanna, Balraj	Holtby (1984)
Kilcommons, Denis	CWA (1987)
Kilroy, Thomas	Booker SL & Guardian (1971)
King, Francis	Maugham (1952), YP (1983)
King, James	YP (1987)
Kneale, Matthew	Trask SL (1986), Maugham (1988)
Kneale, Nigel	Maugham (1950)
Knight, Bernard	Odd (1983)
Knight, Lindsay	MIND (1986)
Knox, Bill	CWA (1986)
Kochan, Lionel	Wingate (1978)
Koliopoulos, John S.	Runciman (1988)
Kuppner, Frank	SAC (1984)
Lamb, Richard	YP (1983)
Lambert, Nina	RNA (1987)
Lamming, George	Maugham (1957)
Lamming, R. M.	Higham (1983)
Larkin, Philip	Smith (1984)
Larner, Christina	SAC (1982)
Lathen, Emma	CWA (1967)
Lavin, Mary	Black (1943)
Lawrence, D. H.	Black (1920)
le Carré, John	CWA (1964), Maugham (1964), Black & CWA (1977)
Leach, Christopher	Pen (1973/4)
Leapman, Michael	Cook (1983)
Leather, John	King (1970)
Lee, Laurie	Smith (1960)
Lefebure, Molly	Davies (1988)
Leff, Leonard J.	BFI (1988)
Leigh, James	CWA (1981)
Leitch, Maurice	Guardian (1969), Whitbread (1981)
Leonard, Tom	Saltire (1984)
Lessing, Doris	Maugham (1954), Booker SL (1971, 1981 & 1985), Smith (1986)
Levey, Michael	Hawthornden (1968), London (1987)
Levi, Peter	Southern (1983)

Author Index

Lewin, Roger	Science (1989)
Lewin, Ronald	Smith (1977)
Lewis, Alun	Rhys (1944)
Lewis, Norman	Angel (1984)
Lindsay, Frederic	SAC (1988)
Linklater, Andro	SAC (1987)
Lister, Ruth	Odd (1978)
Littell, Robert	CWA (1973)
Litvinof, Emanuel	Wingate (1979)
Lively, Penelope	Whitbread (1976), Booker SL (1977), Southern (1978), Booker SL (1984), Booker (1987)
Llewellyn-Williams, Hilary	WAC (1988)
Lochhead, Liz	SAC (1984)
Lodge, David	Hawthornden & YP (1975), Whitbread (1980), Booker SL (1984), Booker SL & Express (1988)
Lofts, Norah	Historical (1979)
Longford, Elizabeth	Black (1964), YP (1969)
Lovesey, Peter	CWA (1978 & 1982)
Lowe-Watson, Dawn	Authors (1980), Elgin (1983)
Lowy, Simon	Bartlett (1979)
Lubbock, Percy	Black (1922)
Lucie-Smith, Edward	Rhys (1962)
Lyall, Gavin	CWA (1965)
Lynch, Michael	SAC (1982)
Lyons, F. S. L.	RSL (1977)
Mabey, Richard	Whitbread (1986)
Macarthur, Catherine	RNA (1978)
Macaulay, Rose	Black (1956)
Macbeth, George	Faber (1964), Angel (1987)
McCabe, Brian	SAC (1984, 1985 & 1987)
McCabe, Eugene	Holtby (1976)
MacCaig, Norman	SAC (1984), Saltire (1985), SAC (1986 & 1988)
McCarthy, Thomas	Bartlett (1981)
McCaughrean, Geraldine	Whitbread (1987)
McClure, James	CWA (1971 & 1976)
Maccoll, D. S.	Black (1945)
McDonald, Alan	Odd (1986)
McDonald, Anne	MIND (1982)
Macdonald, Lyn	SAC (1983), YP (1987)
Macdonald, Ross	CWA (1965)

Author Index

Macdonald, Sheila	Whitbread (1977)
Macdonell, A. G.	Black (1933)
McEwan, Ian	Booker SL (1981), Whitbread (1987)
McGee, Harold	Simon (1986)
Macgregor, David	King (1973)
McGuckian, Medbh	Bartlett (1982)
McGuiness, Frank	Cheltenham (1986)
McIlvanney, William	Faber (1967), Whitbread (1975), CWA (1977 & 1983)
Macintyre, Alex	Boardman (1984)
Mackay, Colin	SAC (1986)
Mackay, Shena	Fawcett (1987)
McKee, Alisdair	Trask (1989)
Mackenzie, Jeanne	RSL (1977), YP (1979)
Mackenzie, Norman	RSL (1977), YP (1979)
Mackie, Alastair	SAC (1987)
Mackinnon, John	YP SL (1974)
McKnight, Hugh	Cook (1984)
MacLaverty, Bernard	SAC (1981, 1982 & 1983), McVitie's & SAC (1988)
Maclean, Alasdair	SAC (1984)
Maclean, Cailean	SAC (1986)
Maclean, Sorley	SAC (1986)
McLeod, Enid	Cooper (1970)
Macleod, Sheila	MIND (1981)
McLynn, F. J. M.	Cheltenham (1985)
McNab, Tom	SAC (1982)
McWilliam, Candida	SAC & Trask (1988)
Madden, Deirdre	Maugham (1989)
Maddocks, Margaret	RNA (1976)
Maddox, Brenda	Pen (1989)
Maher, Barbara	Simon (1982)
Mainstone, Rowland J.	Runciman (1989)
Maitland, Sara	Maugham (1979)
Malet, Oriel	Rhys (1946)
Mann, William	YP (1982)
Manning, Olivia	YP (1977)
Mantel, Hilary	Express SL (1988)
Manton, Jo	Southern (1986)
Mare, Walter de la	Black (1921)
Mark, Jan	Angel (1987)
Markish, David	Wingate (1977)
Marnham, Patrick	Cook (1985)
Mars-Jones, Adam	Maugham (1982)

Author Index

Marshall, Peter	Rhys (1963)
Martin, Alex	Trask (1988)
Martin, Rhona	Historical (1978)
Martin, Robert Bernard	Black, Cooper & RSL (1980)
Masefield, Richard	YP SL (1983)
Mason, Anita	Booker SL (1983)
Mason, Philip	YP (1974)
Mason, Richard	Rhys (1948)
Massie, Alan	SAC (1982 & 1987)
Masters, Anthony	Rhys (1967)
Masters, Brian	CWA (1985)
Mathias, Roland	WAC (1972 & 1980)
Matthews, Denis	YP (1985)
Mauger, David	Odd (1979)
Mavor, Elizabeth	Booker SL (1973)
Maw, James	Trask (1987)
May, Steve	TSB (1988)
Mays, Spike	YP (1969)
Mear, Robert	Boardman (1987)
Meredith, Christopher	WAC (1985)
Merrill, John	YP (1987)
Merritt, Giles	Odd (1982)
Messinger, Gary	Portico (1985)
Meyer, Michael	Whitbread (1971)
Meyer, Nicholas	CWA (1975)
Michel, Freda	RNA (1975)
Mickelburgh, Edwin	McVitie's (1988)
Middleton, Christopher	Faber (1964)
Middleton, Stanley	Booker (1974)
Miller, Christine	SAC (1982)
Miller, John	Pen (1988)
Miller, Karl	Black (1975)
Milne, James Leigh	RSL (1981)
Milne, John	Rhys (1985)
Milne, Roseleen	Elgin (1977)
Minhinnick, Robert	WAC (1980 & 1984)
Mitchell, Alice	Trask SL (1985)
Mitchell, Elma	SAC (1988)
Mitchell, Julian	Rhys (1965), Maugham (1966)
Mo, Timothy	Faber (1979), Booker SL & Hawthornden (1982), Booker SL (1986)
Montague, John	Bartlett (1978)
Moorcock, Michael	Guardian (1977)

Moore, Brian	Authors (1955), Smith (1973), Black (1975), Booker SL (1976), RSL (1985), Booker SL & Express (1987)
Moore, Katherine	Authors (1983)
Moorehead, Alan	Cooper (1956)
Moorhouse, Geoffrey	Cook (1984)
Moorman, Mary	Black (1965)
Moorsom, Sasha	Authors, YP SL (1976)
Moraes, Dom	Hawthornden (1958)
Morgan, Alison	WAC (1973)
Morgan, Charles	Hawthornden (1932), Black (1940)
Morgan, Edwin	Saltire (1983), SAC (1985 & 1988)
Morgan, Kenneth	WAC (1976 & 1982)
Morley, John David	YP (1985)
Morrice, Ken	SAC (1982)
Morris, G. H.	Constable (1986)
Morris, Ivan	Cooper (1964)
Morris, Jan	Booker SL (1985)
Morris, Richard	YP SL (1979)
Morrison, Blake	Maugham (1985)
Mortimer, Chapman	Black (1951)
Mortimer, John	YP (1982)
Mortimer, Penelope	Whitbread (1979)
Moses, D.	SCSE (1985)
Mosley, Nicholas	Booker SL (1969)
Moss, Michael S.	Simon (1981)
Mossman, James	Authors (1965/6)
Motion, Andrew	Rhys (1984), Maugham (1987)
Mottram, Ralph Hale	Hawthornden (1924)
Moule, C. F. D.	Collins (1977)
Moynagh, Michael	Odd (1985)
Muldoon, Paul	Faber (1982)
Munro, Alice	Booker SL (1980)
Murdoch, Iris	Booker SL & YP (1969), Booker SL (1970), Black & Booker SL (1973), Whitbread (1974), Booker (1978), Booker SL (1985 & 1987)
Murray, Annabel	RNA (1982)
Murray, Frances	Elgin & RNA (1974)
Myers, L. H.	Black (1935)
Naipaul, Shiva	Rhys (1971), Whitbread (1973)
Naipaul, V. S.	Rhys (1958), Maugham (1961), Hawthornden (1964), Smith (1968), Booker (1971), Booker SL (1979)

Author Index

Nairn, Tom	Saltire (1988)
Namier, Julia	Black (1971)
Naughton, Bill	Portico (1987)
Neale, J. E.	Black (1934)
Neel, Janet	CWA (1988)
Neilan, Sarah	Elgin (1976)
Neill, William	SAC (1985)
Newby, P. H.	Maugham (1948), YP (1968), Booker (1969)
Newman, Nanette	Bejam (1986)
Newsome, David	Whitbread (1980)
Nicolson, Adam	Maugham (1986)
Nicolson, Harold	YP (1967)
Nicolson, Louise	London (1988)
Nicolson, Nigel	Whitbread (1977)
Nkosi, Lewis	Pen (1987)
Noakes, David	Black (1985)
Nolan, Christopher	Whitbread (1987)
Nonhebel, Clare	Trask (1984)
Noone, John	Faber (1967)
Norris, Christopher	WAC (1986)
Norris, Leslie	Bartlett (1970), WAC (1975), Higham (1978), WAC (1979)
Norwich, John Julius	YP (1981)
Nye, Robert	Guardian & Hawthornden (1976)
O'Brien, Conor Cruse	Wingate (1986)
O'Brien, Edna	YP (1970)
O'Brien, Kate	Black & Hawthornden (1931)
O'Brien, Sean	Maugham (1984)
O'Casey, Sean	Hawthornden (1925)
O'Faolain, Julia	Booker SL (1980)
O'Flaherty, Liam	Black (1925)
Oman, Carola	Black (1953)
Ommaney, F. D.	Pen (1971)
Onions, G. Oliver	Black (1946)
Oram, H. R.	King (1974)
Ordnance Survey	Davies (1984)
Ormond, John	WAC (1970 & 1974)
Osborne, Charles	YP (1981)
Owens, Agnes	SAC (1984)
Owens, Philip	WAC (1980)
Oz, Amos	Wingate (1988)

Author Index

Page, Martin	Authors (1979)
Painter, George	Cooper (1965), Black (1977)
Pakenham, Thomas	Cheltenham (1980)
Paretsky, Sara	CWA (1988)
Parker, Merren	Odd (1979)
Parkes, Tim	Maugham, Rhys & Trask (1986)
Parnell, Michael	YP (1984)
Paton-Walsh, Jill	Whitbread (1974)
Patterson, Glenn	Trask SL (1988)
Paulin, Tom	Maugham (1978), Faber (1982)
Pearce, Philippa	Whitbread (1978)
Pearson, John	Authors (1962)
Peate, Iowerth	WAC (1973)
Peckham, Audrey	MIND (1985)
Peppercorn, David	Simon (1982)
Percy, Lord Eustace	Black (1937)
Perrin, Jim	Boardman (1985)
Peters, Ellis	CWA (1980)
Phillips, N. R.	TSB (1987)
Phillips, Roger	Simon (1983)
Pick, J. B.	SAC (1982)
Pickthall, Barry	King SL (1985)
Pilcher, Rosamund	Elgin (1988)
Pimlott, Ben	Whitbread (1985)
Pinney, Lucy	Trask SL (1987)
Pitter, Ruth	Hawthornden (1937)
Plomer, William	Whitbread (1973)
Pollock, Linda	SCSE (1982/3)
Pollock, Rachel	Clarke (1988)
Polunin, Miriam	Bejam (1985)
Ponsonby of Shulbrede, Lord	Black (1942)
Pope, Dudley	King (1977)
Pope-Hennessy, James	Hawthornden (1940), Whitbread (1972)
Porter, Peter	Cooper (1983), Whitbread (1988)
Porter, Ruth	Odd (1984)
Post, Laurens van der	YP (1967)
Pow, Tom	SAC (1987)
Powell, Anthony	Black (1957), Smith (1974)
Powell, Lily	Black (1970)
Powell, Michael	BFI (1987)
Prescott, Hilda F. M.	Black (1940)
Price, Anthony	CWA (1970 & 1974)
Price, Marion	Fawcett (1982)

Author Index

Priestley, J. B.	Black (1929)
Prince, Peter	Maugham (1973)
Pritchett, V. S.	Pen (1973/4)
Profumo, David	Faber (1989)
Pryce-Jones, David	Whitbread (1986)
Pugh, Sheenagh	WAC (1988)
Purseglove, Jeremy	Kent (1988/9)
Purves, Libby	King (1985)
Pybus, Rodney	Bartlett (1973)
Pym, Barbara	Booker SL & Southern (1977)
Raban, Jonathan	Cook & RSL (1981), King SL (1986)
Rackham, Oliver	Angel (1986)
Raine, Craig	Southern (1979)
Raine, Kathleen	Smith (1972)
Ransford, Tessa	SAC (1981)
Raphael, Chaim	Wingate (1983)
Ratcliff, Ruth	SAC (1984)
Rathbone, Julian	Booker SL (1976 & 1979)
Raven, C. E.	Black (1947)
Raworth, Tom	Bartlett (1969)
Rayner, Richard	Express SL (1988)
Raz, Joseph	Mackenzie (1986)
Read, Piers Paul	Faber (1969), Hawthornden & Maugham (1970)
Reading, Peter	Whitbread (1986)
Redgrove, Peter	Guardian (1973)
Redmon, Anne	YP (1974)
Reed, Jeremy	Maugham (1985)
Rees, Simon	Trask SL (1984)
Reid, Christopher	Hawthornden & Maugham (1980)
Reid, Forrest	Black (1944)
Renault, Mary	Pen (1971)
Rendell, Ruth	Angel (1984), CWA (1976, 1984 & 1986)
Reynolds, Oliver	WAC (1986 & 1988)
Rhys, Jean	Smith (1967)
Rhys, John Llewellyn	Hawthornden (1942)
Richards, Alun	WAC (1974)
Richards, Eric	SAC (1982)
Richardson, Robert	CWA (1985)
Richey, Michael	Rhys (1942)
Richler, Mordecai	Booker SL (1971), Wingate (1981)
Ridley, Jasper	Black (1970)

Author Index

Rietschoten, Cornelius van	King SL (1985)
Riviere, William	Trask (1989)
Robertson, Denise	Constable (1984)
Robinson, David	Machell (1986)
Robinson, Jancis	Simon (1986)
Robinson, Peter	Cheltenham (1988)
Roche, Paul	Bartlett (1966)
Rogers, Jane	Maugham (1985)
Rose, Kenneth	Whitbread & YP (1983)
Ross, Maggie	Black (1968)
Ross, Ronald	Black (1923)
Rowan, Hester	RNA (1976)
Rowe, Dorothy	MIND (1983)
Royle, Trevor	SAC (1983)
Rubens, Bernice	Booker (1970), WAC (1976), Booker SL (1978), WAC (1988)
Rubin, David	Authors (1963)
Rumens, Carol	Bartlett (1981)
Runciman, Sir Stephen	Pen (1969)
Rush, Christopher	SAC (1983 & 1985)
Rushdie, Salman	Black & Booker (1981), Booker SL (1983), Booker SL & Whitbread (1988)
Rushforth, P. S.	Hawthornden (1979)
Russell, Philippa	Odd (1984)
Rutter, Michael	Odd (1979)
Sacks, Oliver	Hawthornden (1974)
Sackville-West, Edward	Black (1936)
Sackville-West, Victoria	Hawthornden (1926 & 1933)
Salter, Brian J.	SCSE (1985)
Sanderson, Margaret H.B.	SAC (1987)
Sassoon, Siegfried	Black & Hawthornden (1928)
Saunders, Kate	Trask SL (1986)
Sayer, Paul	Constable & Whitbread (1988)
Scammell, Michael	Pen (1986)
Scarisbrick, J. J.	YP (1968)
Schickel, Richard	BFI (1985)
Schlee, Anne	Booker SL (1981)
Scholes, Percy A.	Black (1948)
Schweiz, George	Trask SL (1985)
Scimone, Guiseppi	London (1987)
Scott, David	Faber (1986)
Scott, Doug	Boardman (1984)

Author Index

Scott, Geoffrey	Black (1925)
Scott, Paul	YP (1971), Booker (1977)
Seldon, Anthony	YP SL (1981)
Senior, Olive	Commonwealth (1987)
Serafin, David	CWA (1979)
Serge, Dan Vittorio	Whitbread (1987)
Seth, Vikram	Cook (1983), Bartlett (1985)
Severin, Tim	King (1978), Cook & King (1982)
Shanks, Edward	Hawthornden (1919)
Shaw, Frances J.	SAC (1981)
Shaw, Robert	Hawthornden (1962)
Shepherd, Naomi	Whitbread (1984)
Sigsworth, A.	SCSE (1987)
Silkin, Jon	Faber (1966)
Sillitoe, Alan	Authors (1958), Hawthornden (1960)
Simey, Margaret	Portico (1988)
Simon, Roger L.	CWA (1974)
Simpson, Dorothy	CWA (1985)
Simpson, Helen	Black (1932)
Simpson, Joe	Boardman (1988), NCR (1989)
Sinclair, Andrew	Maugham (1967)
Sinclair, Clive	Maugham (1981)
Skinner, Martyn	Hawthornden (1944)
Slaughter, Carolyn	Faber (1977)
Slee, Peter	SCSE (1986)
Sleightholme, Joyce D.	King (1976)
Smalley, Peter	Rhys (1973)
Smith, Anne	Authors & SAC (1981)
Smith, David	WAC (1981)
Smith, Dennis Mack	Cooper (1976)
Smith, Emma	Black & Rhys (1949)
Smith, Iain Crichton	Pen (1971), SAC (1982)
Smith, Martin Cruz	CWA (1981)
Smyth, Alfred	SAC (1985)
Snow, C. P.	Black (1954), Booker SL (1974)
Soames, Mary	YP (1979)
Spalding, Ruth	Whitbread (1975)
Spark, Muriel	Black & YP (1965), Booker SL (1969 & 1981), Saltire (1987)
Spillard, Anne	YP (1987)
Spurling, Hilary	Cooper & RSL (1984)
Stacey, Margaret	Fawcett (1982)
Stacey, Tom	Rhys (1954)
Stalker, John	Portico (1988)

Author Index

Stallworthy, Jon	Cooper (1974), Smith (1975)
Stassinopoulos, Arianna	YP SL (1973)
Steed, Neville	CWA (1986)
Steedman, Carolyn	Fawcett (1984)
Stern, Vivien	Odd (1987)
Stickland, Caroline	Trask SL (1985)
Storey, David	Rhys (1961), Maugham (1963), Booker SL (1972), Faber (1973), Booker (1976)
Stout, Rex	CWA (1969)
Strachey, Lytton	Black (1921)
Strathern, Paul	Maugham (1973)
Street, Jonathan	Maugham (1973)
Strong, L. A. G.	Black (1945)
Sutherland, Allan T.	Odd (1981)
Swan, Robert	Boardman (1987)
Sweetland, Magda	Authors (1985)
Swift, Graham	Booker SL, Faber, Guardian & Holtby (1983)
Sykes, Christopher Simon	London (1986)
Symons, Julian	CWA (1957)
Szirtes, George	Faber (1980)
Tabarlay, Eric	King (1971)
Tapper, T.	SCSE (1985)
Taylor, Andrew	CWA (1982), Whitbread (1986)
Taylor, Bernard	CWA (1987)
Taylor, Elizabeth	Booker SL (1971)
Taylor, John V.	Collins (1973)
Terán, Lisa St Aubin de	Maugham & Rhys (1983)
Terraine, John	YP (1985)
Theroux, Paul	Whitbread (1978), Black & YP (1981), Hawthornden (1988), Cook (1989)
Thomas, D. M.	Booker SL & Cheltenham (1981), Pen (1982)
Thomas, Frances	WAC (1987)
Thomas, Hugh	Maugham (1962)
Thomas, Peter	WAC (1987)
Thomas, R. S.	WAC (1973 & 1976)
Thomas, Rosie	RNA (1985)
Thomson, David	McVitie's (1987), NCR (1988)
Thomson, Derick	Saltire (1983)
Thomson, George Malcolm	YP (1964)
Thorneycroft, Lord	YP (1985)

Author Index

Thornton, Peter	Davies (1986/7)
Thorold, Henry	Cook (1985)
Thubron, Colin	Pen (1985), Cook (1988)
Thwaite, Ann	Cooper (1985)
Timerman, Jacob	CWA (1981)
Tindall, Gillian	Elgin (1970), Maugham (1972)
Tinniswood, Peter	Authors (1969), WAC (1975)
Tinsley, Nina	RNA (1980)
Tomalin, Claire	Whitbread (1973), NCR SL (1988)
Torrance, Thomas F.	Collins (1969)
Tremain, Rose	Angel (1985)
Trench, Richard	London (1985)
Trench, Sally	YP SL (1968)
Trevelyan, G. M.	Black (1920)
Trevor, Meriol	Black (1962)
Trevor, William	Hawthornden (1965), Booker SL (1970), RSL (1975), Booker SL & Whitbread (1976), Whitbread (1983)
Trickett, Rachel	Rhys (1953)
Trollope, Joanna	RNA (1980)
Tuohy, Frank	Black (1964), Faber (1965), RSL (1978)
Turnbull, Gael	Bartlett (1968)
Turner, Chris	London (1985)
Turner, George	Clarke (1987), Commonwealth SL (1988)
Turow, Scott	CWA (1987)
Tynan, Kathleen	NCR SL (1988)
Underwood, John	Cook (1989)
Underwood, Pat	Cook (1989)
Unsworth, Barry	Booker SL (1980)
Unwin, David	Authors (1954)
Vanderhaeghe, Guy	Faber (1987)
Vanstone, W. H.	Collins (1979)
Vat, Dan van der	YP SL (1982), King (1983)
Vaughan, Matthew	Higham (1975)
Venables, Stephen	Boardman (1986)
Vernon, Francis	Authors (1982)
Vettese, Raymond	Saltire (1988)
Vine, Barbara	CWA (1987), Angel (1988)
Virtue, Noel	Express SL (1987)
Vital, David	Wingate (1982)

Wain, John	Maugham (1958), Black (1974), Whitbread (1982)
Wainwright, Alfred	Davies (1985)
Walcott, Derek	RSL (1982)
Waley, Arthur	Black (1942)
Walker, Alan	Black & YP (1983)
Walker, Ted	Bartlett (1967), Ackerley (1983)
Wallace, Marjorie	Odd (1986)
Walpole, Hugh	Black (1919)
Walsh, Sheila	RNA (1974 & 1984)
Walters, Anne-Marie	Rhys (1947)
Warburg, Tessa Lorant	Odd (1988)
Ward, Aileen	Cooper (1963)
Ward, Colin	Angel (1985)
Ward, Edmund	Authors (1957)
Ward, J. P.	WAC (1985)
Warner, Marina	Fawcett (1986), Booker SL (1988), Pen (1989)
Warner, Rex	Black (1960)
Wasserstein, Bernard	CWA (1988)
Waterhouse, Keith	Express SL (1988)
Watson, Peter	CWA (1983)
Watson, William	SAC (1983)
Watts, Nigel	Trask (1989)
Waugh, Evelyn	Hawthornden (1936), Black (1952)
Webb, Harri	WAC (1970)
Webster, Susan	Trask SL (1988)
Wedgewood, C. V.	Black (1944)
Weldon, Fay	Booker SL (1979)
Wells, John	King SL (1987)
Wells, Nigel	WAC (1981)
Welsh, Frank	King SL (1988)
Wesley, Mary	Express SL (1987)
West, Maurice	Black (1959)
West, Rebecca	YP (1966)
Weston, Michael	Historical (1986)
Weyer, Robert van der	Stanford (1988)
Whale, John	Stanford (1980)
Wheeler, T.	Booker SL (1970)
White, Jerry	Wingate (1981)
White, Patrick	Smith (1959)
Whitnell, Barbara	Elgin (1984)
Whitworth, John	Bartlett (1980)
Wiles, John	Rhys (1955)

Author Index

Wiles, Maurice	Collins (1983)
Wilkins, Eithne	YP SL (1969)
Wilks, Ivor	WAC (1985)
Willan, Anne	Simon (1981)
Willard, Barbara	Whitbread (1984)
Williams, G. M.	Booker SL (1969)
Williams, Gareth	WAC (1981)
Williams, Glanmor	WAC (1988)
Williams, Gwyn A.	WAC (1977)
Williams, Gwyn Alfred	WAC (1979)
Williams, Hugo	Faber (1980)
Williams, John Stuart	WAC (1971)
Williams, Nigel	Maugham (1978)
Williams, Raymond	WAC (1980, 1986)
Williamson, Duncan	SAC (1987)
Williamson, Henry	Hawthornden (1927)
Williamson, Linda	SAC (1987)
Wilson, A. N.	Rhys (1978), Southern (1980), Maugham & Rhys (1981), Smith (1983), Whitbread (1988), NCR (1989)
Wilson, Angus	Black (1958), YP (1970)
Wilson, John	Whitbread (1973)
Wilson, Nelly	Wingate (1979)
Wilson, Romer	Hawthornden (1921)
Wilson, William	Black (1924)
Winterson, Jeanette	Whitbread (1985), Rhys (1987)
Woodall, Corbet	Odd (1980)
Woodham-Smith, Cecil	Black (1950)
Woolf, Leonard	Smith (1965)
Worboys, Anne	Elgin (1975), RNA (1977)
Workman, H. B.	Black (1926)
Wormald, Jeremy	SAC (1981)
Wright, Hannah	Simon (1985)
Wright, Kit	Bartlett (1977), Faber (1978)
Wright, Patricia	Historical (1987)
Wright, Richard	Faber (1975)
Wurman, R.	London (1987)
Wyndham, Francis	Whitbread (1987)
Yadin, Yigael	Wingate (1985)
Yallop, David	CWA (1984)
Yan-Kit, So	Simon (1984)
Yehoshua, A. B.	Wingate (1980)
Yorke, Matthew	Rhys (1988)

Author Index

Young, Andrew — Cooper (1960)
Young, E. H. — Black (1930)
Young, Francis Brett — Black (1927)
Young, G. M. — Black (1952)

Zameenzad, Adam — Higham (1987)
Ziegler, Philip — RSL (1976)

Subject Index

Biography	J. R. Ackerley Prize
	James Tait Black Memorial Prize
	Duff Cooper Memorial Prize
	Hawthornden Prize
	Nelson Hurst and Marsh Biography Award
	McVitie's Prize for the Scottish Writer of the Year
	John Llewellyn Rhys Memorial Prize
	Royal Society of Literature Award under the W. H. Heinemann Bequest
	W. H. Smith Literary Award
	Whitbread Literary Awards
*Children's literature	Whitbread Literary Awards
Education	SCSE Book Prizes
Environment	Sir Peter Kent Conservation Book Prize
Fiction see also specific categories of fiction	Angel Literary Prize
	James Tait Black Memorial Prize
	Booker Prize
	Cheltenham Prize
	Commonwealth Writers' Prize
	Constable Trophy
	Geoffrey Faber Memorial Prize
	Fawcett Society Book Prize
	Guardian Fiction Prize
	Hawthornden Prize
	Winifred Holtby Memorial Prize
	McVitie's Prize for the Scottish Writer of the Year
	Somerset Maugham Award
	John Llewellyn Rhys Memorial Prize

(* the only children's literature award included)

Subject Index

	Royal Society of Literature Award under the W. H. Heinemann Bequest
	Saltire Society and *The Scotsman* Literary Awards
	Scottish Arts Council Book Awards
	Silver Pen Awards
	W. H. Smith Literary Award
	Southern Arts Literature Prize
	Sunday Express Book of the Year
	Betty Trask Awards
	TSB Peninsula Prize
	Welsh Arts Council Prizes
	Whitbread Literary Awards
	H. H. Wingate Prize
	Yorkshire Post Awards
Crime fiction	Crime Writers' Association Awards
First novel	Author's Club First Novel Award
	Crime Writers' Association Awards
	David Higham Prize for Fiction
	Romantic Novelists Association Awards
	Saltire Society and *The Scotsman* Literary Award
	Betty Trask Awards
	Whitbread Literary Awards
	Yorkshire Post Awards
Historical fiction	Historical Novel Prize in Memory of Georgette Heyer
Romantic fiction	Mary Elgin Award
	Romantic Novelists Association Awards
	Betty Trask Awards
Science fiction	Arthur C. Clarke Award
Food and drink	Bejam Cookery Book of the Year
	André Simon Memorial Fund Book Awards
History	Duff Cooper Memorial Prize
	Royal Society of Literature Award under the W. H. Heinemann Bequest

Subject Index

Media and the arts	British Film Institute Book Award Roger Machell Prize *Yorkshire Post* Awards
Non-fiction see also specific subjects	Angel Literary Prize Cheltenham Prize Crime Writers' Association Non-Fiction Award Hawthornden Prize Winifred Holtby Memorial Prize McVitie's Prize for the Scottish Writer of the Year NCR Book Award for Non-Fiction Portico Prize John Llewellyn Rhys Memorial Prize Royal Society of Literature Award under the W. H. Heinemann Bequest Runciman Award Saltire Society and *The Scotsman* Literary Award Scottish Arts Council Book Awards Silver Pen Awards W. H. Smith Literary Award Somerset Maugham Award Southern Arts Literature Prize Welsh Arts Council Awards H. H. Wingate Prize *Yorkshire Post* Awards
Poetry and drama	Alice Hunt Bartlett Award Duff Cooper Memorial Prize Geoffrey Faber Memorial Prize Hawthornden Prize McVitie's Prize for the Scottish Writer of the Year John Llewellyn Rhys Memorial Prize Royal Society of Literature Award under the W. H. Heinemann Bequest Saltire Society and *The Scotsman* Literary Award Scottish Arts Council Book Awards W. H. Smith Literary Award Somerset Maugham Award Southern Arts Literature Prize Welsh Arts Council Awards Whitbread Literary Awards

Subject Index

Regional	Angel Literary Prize (East Anglia) Constable Trophy (North of England) Hunter Davies Prize for the Lakeland Book of the Year (Lakeland) Winifred Holtby Memorial Prize (regional) London Tourist Board Guide Book of the Year Award (London) McVitie's Prize for the Scottish Writer of the Year (Scotland) Portico Prize (North West England) Saltire Society and *The Scotsman* Literary Award (Scotland) Scottish Arts Council Book Awards (Scotland) Southern Arts Literature Prize (Southern England) TSB Peninsula Prize (South West England) Welsh Arts Council Awards (Wales)
Religion	Collins Religious Book Award Winifred Mary Stanford Prize H. H. Wingate Prize
Science	Science Book Prize
Social and political concerns	Duff Cooper Memorial Prize Fawcett Society Book Prize Mackenzie Prize MIND Book of the Year Odd Fellows (Manchester Unity) Social Concern Book Award
Travel and leisure	Boardman Tasker Memorial Award for Mountain Literature Thomas Cook Travel and Guide Book Awards Hunter Davies Prize for the Lakeland Book of the Year King George's Fund for Sailors Book of the Sea Award London Tourist Board Guide Book of the Year Awards Runciman Award

Bibliography

The books listed below are a source of information for prizes and awards not included in this guide.

Children's books in print 1987–1988 ed. Bowker, 1987.
ISBN 0-8352-2360-4. Lists winners of children's literature awards 1980–1986.

Centre for Children's Books: *Children's book prizes.* National Book League, 1984. ISBN 0-85353-387-3. Lists the winners of the UK children's literature awards to 1983. Available from the Book Trust.

Guide to literary prizes, grants and awards in Britain and Ireland. 5th ed. Book Trust & The Society of Authors, 1988. ISBN 0-85353-418-7. A list of UK and Republic of Ireland awards, grants and fellowships for adult and children's literature.

Kromer, Martin: *Pick of the year*. Federation of Children's Book Groups. (Regularly updated). Lists the winner of the Children's Book Award and other recommended books tried and tested by children. Available from the Federation of Children's Book Groups, 22 Beacon Row, Bradford BD5 3DE.

O. S. Weber & S. J. Calvert: *Literary and library prizes*. 8th ed. Bowker, 1980. ISBN 0-8352-1249-1. Lists the winners of the major UK, US, Canadian and European literary awards.

Useful Addresses

BOOK TRUST
Book House, 45 East Hill, London SW18 2QZ. Tel. 01-870 9055.
Administers many of the prizes listed in this guide. Produces author profiles and guides to children's and adult literature. Houses the Children's Book Foundation with its extensive library which is open to the public. Also provides a fast and efficient book information service which is free for brief queries.

BOOK TRUST SCOTLAND
15a Lynedoch Street, Glasgow G3 6EF. Tel. (041) 332 0391.
Publishes the *Directory of writers in Scotland*, houses a children's reference library which is open to the public and organizes exhibitions and author talks and seminars.

PUBLISHERS ASSOCIATION
19 Bedford Square, London WC1B 3HJ. Tel. 01-580 6321.
Produces literature guides and special campaigns, e.g. Best Novels of our Time, Best of British Authors and Best of Young British Novelists.